LEARN TO
Love

Guide to Healing Your Disappointing Love Life

THOMAS JORDAN, Ph.D.

This book is dedicated to all the people
I have loved in my life thus far, regardless
of whether or not, they were able or willing
to love me back.

ACKNOWLEDGEMENTS

I am very thankful to all the people who have helped me develop my personal and professional understanding of the love relationship. My wife Victoria Jordan and son Bradley are at the top of my list. I am so grateful for the learning about love relationships that has taken place in my marriage and family. I am also grateful for Bradley's invaluable technical assistance with this book, the Love Life Seminar, and Love Life Webinar.

I am thankful for the teaching my psychoanalyst, the late Dr. Benjamin Wolstein, did on the topic of the love relationship during the course of my psychoanalysis. He passed along an initial understanding of the relationship between learning and the healthy and unhealthy love life that is fundamental to the ideas presented in this book.

I want to thank my dear mother and father for their support and interest in my psychological ideas and research over the years. My late mother, Hilda Jordan, was always interested in the psychology of her own life, and was ready to remind me that she herself was responsible for my passionate interest in psychology and psychoanalysis. She willingly and enthusiastically shared her emotional experience with me, and I am quite sure she would have been honored by the opportunity to be a part of my research on transforming the adult love life. Something she needed but never had the chance to do in her lifetime.

I would also like to thank our good friend Alex Abrams for the inspiration he gave me that originally started this writing project and his editing of the final manuscript. He convinced me that learning about love relationships was insufficiently understood, had to be taught, and a book was one the best ways to start spreading the word.

I would also like to thank the various patients in my practice I have had the honor to know and accompany on their personal journeys over the years. They were instrumental in helping me learn about healthy and unhealthy love relationships.

Lastly, I would like to thank the scores of people who came to the Love Life Learning Center blog to read and learn about the love relationship. Their trials and tribulations as documented in their commentary and discussions provided much of the love life experience used to evolve the ideas presented in this book.

Table of Contents

PART III UNLEARNING METHOD

CONCLUSION

PREFACE

This is not a book about love. This is a book about love relationships. About the relationships we form, healthy or unhealthy, when we fall in love. A healthy relationship nurtures love, an unhealthy one stifles it. Furthermore, the type of relationship you tend to form in love is not something you are born with. It is learned, consciously or not, and it's usually unconsciously learned. That means most of us don't know consciously what we've learned about love relationships.

Here's where it gets really interesting. Consider the divorce rate, around 50% according to the latest statistics. You have a 50/50 chance of getting divorced when you marry, that's considered no better than chance. If the relationship you form when you marry is determined by what you've learned in the course of your life, then, if you found out what you've learned about love relationships, could you then change it and learn something else? Improve your chances of finding and sustaining love beyond just chance?

This question has been on my mind for quite a long time. A long time because I did not have a ready-made answer for it. It took years of clinical research to come up with a tentative understanding and years more to find some of the indisputable facts provided in the pages of this book. The answer to the question, by the way, is a resounding yes. If you know what you've learned about love relationships, you can change it and improve your chances of finding and sustaining a healthy love relationship. Otherwise, what you've learned stays in charge of your love life, unbeknownst to you. The trouble is, a healthy love relationship may not be the objective of what you've learned.

Most of the time we talk about love as a coveted state of mind and heart without an understanding or even an awareness of what it takes to have and hold onto a healthy love relationship. We've relegated love relating to something innately given and taken for granted. We don't bother to think that our love lives like any other important area of our lives has dynamics that are understandable and can be improved upon if necessary. I've learned that a big part of the problem is what we learn about love relationships in the bosom of our family of origin. If you haven't already noticed, it has only been in recent times that our society has had the nerve to question what happens in family life and its connection to how well or unwell we feel. We used to just leave that alone.

Now that the "family of origin" is understood to be a primary source of what we've learned about love relationships and other important topics of interest, we can now take a closer look at this earliest of emotional classrooms and begin to understand what was learned there. Believe me, our purpose is not to aimlessly disrupt this sacred place. But to find the information we'll need to understand and own our own love lives.

Dr. Thomas Jordan
New York City
2019

INTRODUCTION

WHAT IS A LOVE LIFE?

What are the two most intense but normal human emotions? Let's get hate and rage off the table right from the start because neither of them is normal. Given the title of this book as a clue, if you say love you'd have one. The other is grief, which happens to be the true opposite of love. If you love someone you will inevitably grieve. Essentially, grief is the loss of the person you love. If grief is what happens when love leaves, love is a pretty important and far reaching emotion for human beings.

I asked you this question to make a point. Neither of these intense but normal human emotions are the subject of any systematic effort to teach, instruct, train or otherwise inform our young. Yet they remain the focal point of so much distortion, misunderstanding, and illness over the course of a lifetime. Why the oversight? The reasons for this oversight will become clearer to you as you read on.

This book is an effort to fill in this glaring gap concerning the emotion of love. The information in these pages was collected from years of clinical research, the type of research that occurs as a consequence of helping people develop themselves in psychotherapy and psychoanalysis over time (Jordan, 1999). Many of my patients started treatment with love life problems either as the source of their difficulty or as a byproduct.

But let's not get ahead of ourselves. A definition of the phrase "love life" is in order. I'll ask you the question again, "What is a love life?" My definition is: *any and all interpersonal relationships involving the emotion of love, past and present.* There is one important advantage in this particular definition. It defines a love life as including "all" the relationships in your life that involved the emotion of love. Implication being, your love life starts the moment you are born and ends the moment you die. This is precisely why "past and present" are emphasized.

I suggest you keep this definition in mind because the importance of the connection between past and present love relationships is essential to the ideas and method presented in this book.

In the early 1970s, Leo Buscaglia, Ph.D. a professor of education at the University of California at Berkeley, became aware of the suicide death of one of his female students presumably over a love life problem. Moved by this tragic loss, made worse by his recognition of the potential of this particular student, he made a proposal to the administration to teach a "Love Class" at the university. Their initial reaction was to poke fun, criticizing the topic as "unscientific," and suggesting that Dr. Buscaglia had better things to do with his time. His motivation to teach a class on love came from a desire to understand and educate young people on how to better cope with life believing that the experience of love was at the core of this concern.

Dr. Buscaglia persisted in his efforts to teach the class. The university administration finally conceded with the condition that he could use a classroom but the class would be taught without credit. He taught his Love Class for four years with a maximum enrollment of one hundred students each year, standing room only. Dr. Buscaglia was so moved by the students' interest that he tearfully admitted in the first class that he had doubts about having sufficient knowledge to teach about love and would rely upon the possibility of learning together. He subsequently published a number of books presenting what he had learned about love as a consequence of teaching his Love Class (Buscaglia, 1972, 1982, 1984, 1992).

Leo Buscaglia's effort to research and teach about love life considerations in a class was unusual and to my knowledge never replicated. The primary source of his research were the young adult students he encountered at the university and in his Love Class. The love life research I did was conducted over the course of thirty years with a more varied population of people in my private practice in New York City. Many of my patients presented with love life difficulties they struggled to change individually or in a couple therapy with their partners.

Just like Leo Buscaglia learned from his students, I have learned quite a bit from the people I've treated over the years. One important thing I've learned is that love in the form of a love relationship is learned. This book is an effort to present to my readers, in an easily readable form, what can be learned about love relationships, and when necessary what can be done about it when the learning is unhealthy. A circumstance that is too often the case for many of us.

Why is love so difficult?

Finding and sustaining a healthy love relationship is difficult, challenging, sometimes confusing, and too often painful. A 50% divorce rate and the myriad of hurtful relationships and painful breakups that often litter our personal experiences and media make the case. This love life reality and the number of patients showing up at my office suffering from chronic love life problems encouraged me to conduct a bit of clinical research over the course of my 30-year practice to get at the underlying reasons for this difficulty.

In this book I will tell you about my research, what I learned, and what anyone with the motivation to improve their love lives can do about it. By the way, the stakes are pretty high. Imagine living your whole life making the same love life mistakes, without knowing it, over and over again until the prospect of finding a healthy love relationship feels out of reach. Regrettably, this continues to happen to too many people.

The most important message you'll get out of this book is, *love is difficult because the health and success of your love life is determined by what you've learned about love relationships in your life.* The question to ask yourself is, what have I learned about love relationships?

Problem is most people will scratch their heads and say, what? Most people have never considered such a question, let alone answer it.

Without an answer to this question, what you've learned about love relationships will most likely unconsciously repeat itself over and over again, good or bad. In essence, you won't be in control of your love life.

If you've been unfortunate enough to learn something unhealthy about love relationships in your life, chances are pretty good that what you'll be repeating will be love life problems. If you don't know what you've learned, what you'll be repeating will no doubt raise havoc in your love life. This book is a consequence of years of interest in what I like to call "love life psychology." Love life psychology is the study of love lives from the inside out. What I mean is, trying to understand the what, how, and why of a person's love life by studying his or her psychology in the form of beliefs, behavior, and feelings as they play out in love relationships.

I believe, and the clinical evidence substantiates the claim, that most if not all of what happens in an individual's love life can be understood in this way. Recognizing this fact of our psychological existence was exciting to say the least. For years, as a practicing clinical psychologist and psychoanalyst in New York City, I witnessed the pain and suffering caused by an unhealthy love life (Jordan, 2014). For years I applied and experienced the limitations of what I had been trained to believe about love relationships, always wondering if there was more that I could understand and do to help alleviate the pain of an endless number of patients seeking treatment as a result of chronic love life problems. Glad to say, there was and is. It's in the pages of this book.

What will this book teach you?

This book is going to teach you something about your love life that will increase your chances of finding and sustaining a healthy love relationship. There are three parts to this book. Part I is entitled the "Unhealthy Love Life." This is the problem, our nemesis. Understanding how what you've learned about love relationships can result in an out of control unhealthy love life is the place where we'll begin. In this first part of the book, I will tell you everything you'll need to know about how the unhealthy love life, as a noxious force operating beyond your awareness, can limit and disrupt your chances of finding and sustaining a healthy love relationship.

There are two chapters in Part I. Chapter 1, entitled, "My Love Life Research" will discuss four basic characteristics of the unhealthy love life. Understanding these four basic characteristics will strengthen your consciousness, if and when your love life becomes unhealthy. In Chapter 2, entitled, "Learning About Love Relationships" I will discuss the ways we all learn about love relationships, what we learn, and how what we learn can become problematic.

Part II of this book is about the "Psychological Love Life." Chances are you probably didn't think you had one. Surprise, surprise, it turns out that our love life experiences are being shaped, again out of our awareness, from the psychological "backroom," if you will. Your psychological love life is the true "cause" of your love life experiences, healthy or unhealthy. And yes, we all have one.

In Part II of this book I will show you how what you've learned about love relationships is being psychologically used to recreate your "unhealthy relationship experiences." The relationship experiences that originally taught you what you've learned about love relationships in the first place. Becoming aware of your psychological love life will empower you to be able to change what is unhealthy, the focus of the next part of this book. Part II includes Chapter 3, entitled "Your Psychological Love Life." In this chapter we will study the psychological love life as the mental storehouse of what you've learned about love relationships and become familiar with its contents. Becoming aware of what is in your psychological love life gives you access to a part of your emotional life that is usually kept out of awareness as it operates in shaping your love life experiences. Access will permit you to identify what needs to change.

In Part III, I will introduce you to what I call my "Unlearning Method." This is the "solution" to our problem, the unhealthy love life. In this part of the book I'll show you how what you've learned about love relationships can be identified, challenged, and changed. This conscious application of how what was learned, can be unlearned, and something better learned or relearned was taken directly from the successes in my clinical work with patients struggling with love life problems. There are two chapters in Part III of this book.

In Chapter 4, entitled "Changing Your Psychological Love Life" we'll go through each of the 3-steps involved in effectively changing what was learned from unhealthy relationship experiences. In Chapter 5, entitled, "My Psychological Love Life," I apply the Unlearning Method to my own love life experience. What better way to illustrate the effectiveness of this method than to describe how I used it to change my own love life difficulties?

In Chapter 6, I'll review the various ways it is possible to teach about love relationships, both educational and therapeutic. A useful discussion of the various educational and therapeutic formats that are possible to consciously and deliberately teach about love relationships for the purpose of improving your psychological ability to find and sustain a healthy love relationship.

In the "Conclusion" of this book, I will make the case that our objective is to take back, maybe for the very first time, control of our love lives. Your love life is not only what is visible in terms of the people you have loved and love. Your love life is also what is inside of you that shapes and determines the kind of relationships you'll form, and the experiences you will or won't have in love. If and when you become aware of your inside love life, you can switch it from automatic to manual. An old friend used to say, you can't drive your life from the backseat. I think this most certainly applies to your love life.

In its essence this book represents a 21st Century "Love Class." A tribute to Leo Buscaglia's remarkable vision, updated and taken a few steps further. Instead of "Love Class" we'll call it a "Love Relationship Class," since love relationships rather than simply the emotion of love, will remain our primary focus. Consider this book a mini education, derived from years of clinical research, on how we relate in love both healthy and unhealthy, and what we can do about it when it's unhealthy.

PART I
THE UNHEALTHY
LOVE LIFE

CHAPTER 1

My Love Life Research

Types of Unhealthy Love Life

Human beings possess the need to receive and give love. We spend much of our waking hours, consciously or unconsciously, trying to make this happen. At earlier times in our lives, the need to receive love is easier to see, then it tends to go underground. In middle-age it's harder to need love without feeling uncomfortable about it. The need to give love often shows up later in life, even though there are clues to its existence earlier in life. Small children can show extraordinary acts of kindness and love toward others.

We all come into the world with the hope that we'll get and give the love we need. In fact, the relationship between "hope" and love was the first thing I noticed when I began conducting my love life research. My first observation of the unhealthy love life was how the appearance of hope determined the two primary forms of the unhealthy love life. When there is hope, the unhealthy love life will typically take the form of *multiple disappointments.* When a person is struggling with this type of unhealthy love life he or she is trying to find and sustain a healthy love relationship despite multiple disappointments.

People who are experiencing multiple disappointments in love tend to be on the younger end of the age spectrum. The hope of finding and keeping the healthy love relationship they seek is propelling them to keep looking regardless of the hurt their disappointments have caused. At some point or another, this type of unhealthy love life morphs into the second form of unhealthy love life we call *resignation*. When resigned, multiple disappointments have convinced a person that a healthy love relationship is not going to be found. Hope has been lost. The objective now is to live a life without love. Easier said than done.

Some people enter the unhealthy love life state of resignation after only a very few disappointments. In some instances, it only takes one substantial disappointment to swear off love. They decide to stop looking for and getting involved in something that only ends up hurting them. Others are more resilient and continue looking for the love they desire to get and give as many times as possible resisting resignation. Nevertheless, resignation after a period of multiple disappointments with love is for certain. It's only a matter of time. If you are making the same love life mistakes over and over again without awareness, self-preservation in the form of resignation is inevitable.

Repeating Love Life Problems

The second observation we've made about the unhealthy love life is that it is *repetitive*. Whatever love life problem you are experiencing is probably happening over and over again. How many repetitions depends upon your age. There are several forms this repetition can take. Repeating love life problems can occur in a single relationship. For example, a person who cheats in a love relationship several times over the course of the relationship. Repeating love life problems can also occur over the course of several love relationships. Taking the cheating example again, repetition could occur in several different relationships. Then there is the repetition of a past love life problem again in a person's current love relationship. For example, imagine you grew up in a home where your father cheated on your mother, you cheat on your wife, and your son cheats on his wife.

This temporal perspective on repetition in the unhealthy love life was particularly interesting to us. Because we saw it a lot in the relationship experience reported by our patients. Whenever my patients had an unhealthy love life, some form of repetition was usually happening. Furthermore, most people were not aware of it. The frequency of this problem was undeniable. Repeating love life problems you don't know you are repeating. Who or what is in control of our love lives?

Replicating Unhealthy Relationship Experience

Our third observation was that the unhealthy love life *replicates* unhealthy relationship experiences. Upon deeper analysis, repeating love life problems turned out to be replications of a person's previous relationship experiences. It appears that past love life experience is in control of what a person experiences in the present. Little by little, a list of replicating unhealthy relationship experiences started to take shape. The same relationship experiences showed up in different people's love lives, so we began to formulate the idea that certain experiences are naturally "toxic" and commonly repeated and replicated in the adult love life.

To illustrate this idea of "replication" consider the common physical replication that takes place when someone marries someone who looks like his or her mother or father, or some other family member. As if the physical "template," if you will, is unconsciously being used to select someone with "familiar" physical characteristics. Of course, physical replication is only the superficial form of this phenomena, but I think it makes the point. We also took a closer look at the replication of other features in a love relationship like how a love partner behaves, what is believed about love relationships, and how a love partner feels, and found that replications are unconsciously taking place on those levels all the time. Replication is surely taking place in our love lives.

Let's consider a few psychological examples from my clinical work over the years. A woman is abandoned by her father at a young age, survives a controlling mother, and marries a man who abandons her after she gives birth to their children. Her marriage replicates the abandonment she experienced in her family of origin.

A woman grew up in an abusive home where she witnesses her violent alcoholic father abuse her mother. She leaves home and marries a verbally and emotionally abusive man. She replicates the domestic abuse she witnessed growing up now in an emotional and verbal form in her marriage.

A woman grows up in a home where her mother is compulsive and controlling. Her mother controls her father and the children, with her demands for order and organization. She herself gets married and replicates the same learned control over her husband's activities in the home.

A man witnesses the emotional dependency of his father on a controlling mother. He grows up and leaves home, and has two children with a dependent possessive woman who helps him replicate his parents' marriage.

A woman witnesses her mother's emotional pain when her mother discovers that her father is cheating on her. Her mother divorces her father as a consequence of the dishonesty. As an adult she is attracted to men who cannot make a commitment and is chronically suspicious of cheating.

A woman grows up in a family where she feels taken advantage of by her siblings and narcissistic dependent mother. In her adult love life, she struggles in several love relationships with the feeling of being used. She now avoids love life situations to deter an expected exploitation.

A woman grows up in a home with a controlling mother who mistrusts her ability to make her own decisions. She marries the man her mother prefers, takes the job her mother expects her to have, and moves into a home her mother finds for her family. She now struggles with chronic feelings that her life does not belong to her.

A man grew up in a family where his mother neglects him in favor of her husband compelled by the husband's sickness. Her son is left to fend for himself emotionally in the family. He leaves home and finds a neglectful woman with children who focuses predominately on her children replicating the same experience of neglect he endured living with his parents.

A man grows up with a rejecting critical mother and narcissistic distant father. He marries a critical woman and copes with the feeling of hurt by defensively distancing himself in his marriage.

A man grew up with a self-centered mother and self-sacrificing care-taking father. He marries a narcissistic woman and takes care of her in a self-sacrificing manner. He replicates the marital relationship of his parents, taking the role of the depleted care-taker of a self-centered person.

On and on, one example after another, of the "replicated" unhealthy love life. I collected these painful love life stories and many others over the course of many years of practice. Repetition and replication of unhealthy relationship experiences can be found in each instance without any initial awareness of its reoccurrence by the people involved. What remained unclear is why and how this is happening. It was only when I realized that "learning" was the key to understanding the repetition and replication of unhealthy relationship experience, was I then able to go even deeper in my analysis of the unhealthy love life.

CHAPTER 2

Learning About Love Relationships

Recreating Unhealthy Relationship Experiences

We humans are exceptionally creative. Look around, much of the environments we live in have been created by people. The outside world is not the only place we create. We all do quite a bit of creative work on the inside of ourselves as well. The fourth observation we've made of the unhealthy love life is that it *recreates* in the present, past unhealthy relationship experiences with what we've learned previously about love relationships.

Our current relationship experiences are often the recreated experience of whatever happened in the most important interpersonal relationships in our lives. In this case, we are focusing on how we recreate the unhealthy ones. Again, this bit of creative mental work is done without the least bit of consciousness. The most important thing to remember is, *we are using what we've learned about love relationships to do this mental creation.* It basically boils down to recreating what is familiar in our experience of the interpersonal relationships in our lives.

Imagine a painter who paints different subjects in the same motif (e.g. Marco Grassi, Italian painter). Each woman depicted in Grassi's paintings, and there are quite a few, is portrayed in the same colorful surrealistic way. The uniqueness of each woman's face and gesture is preserved, yet the same recreated color theme is replicated in each portrait. To illustrate our concept of recreated love life experience, let's imagine that Grassi is a person who has learned to recreate the same relationship experience in his love life (depicted by the surrealistic color theme) regardless of the woman he falls in love with. What he has learned about relationships is in control of his love life. More specifically, what he has learned about love relationships determines how he relates to each woman he falls in love with.

Love Life Formula

Finding out just how we do this recreation was very compelling to us. What are the learning principles involved? Let's start off with what I like to call the Love Life Formula: *Love Life = Relationships + Love.*

Remember our definition of Love Life as any and all relationships involving the emotion of love, past and present. "Relationships" in this formula is a learned and fairly predictable phenomenon. We essentially learn how to relate from the people who relate to us, or we witness relating to each other, mostly earlier in life.

Love Life = Relationships + Love

"Love," on the other hand, is not learned and is essentially an unpredictable psychological, biological, interpersonal, and spiritual phenomenon. Since love is beyond learning, it's really not my concern in this research. Love can occur, even multiple times, in the average lifetime. Whether or not the relationships we form are healthy enough to nurture and sustain the love we feel when we fall in love is the primary focus of my work.

How Were You Taught About Love?

There are three ways that you can learn about love relationships. The first is by being in a *relationship* with someone. For example, how you are treated in a love relationship will inevitably teach you valuable lessons about love relationships. Quite simply, if you were related to in a healthy way in your love relationships, chances are you'll learn healthy things about love relationships. And vice versa, if you were related to in an unhealthy way, you'll learn unhealthy things about love relationships. This would be true from the very beginning of your life.

The second way you might learn about love relationships is through *observation.* Imagine you are a child growing up in a family where one parent mistreats the other. What you witness between them will teach you things about love in a relationship. In fact, much of what we learn occurs in this way. Again, without the slightest bit of awareness that we are learning by observation.

The last way in which you could learn about love relationships is through *instruction.* This method might be a little harder to imagine since it tends to occur less often than relationship and observation. It's not instruction in the traditional sense of a teacher giving a lecture while students take notes and learn. This instruction would be a bit more insidious. Instructions on love relationships conveyed through the sharing of beliefs or giving guidance about love relationships. As children we are occasionally taught about love relationships by the people we love when telling stories. Love relationship stories are a common way of teaching the young about love.

The best example I have of love relationship instruction occurred in 1961 when I was 8 years old. The family scene is "Waffle Sunday" and my father has the waffle iron on the dining room table making waffles with my mother. My two older brothers and I are sitting around the table while my father makes and my mother serves the waffles. While doing so, my father takes the opportunity to deliver a few love life lessons to his young audience avidly listening in anticipation of the next batch of waffles. My father says, pleased with my mother's help serving the delicious waffles, "when you guys grow up and get married make sure you find a *virgin* like your mother." Upon hearing this pronouncement stated for the benefit of educating the kids, my mother simply smiled without saying a word. Looking back, there is quite an assumption being served as well, that a *good wife is a virgin*. Age and experience have luckily challenged our father's limited anachronistic view of women, permitting his sons to avoid the unhealthy implications of this instruction. The point is, this was a very powerful learning moment at a time in my life when there was little experience to truly understand the particulars of what we were being taught.

Unconscious Learning About Love Relationships

Our ability to learn is our greatest asset, although much if not most of the learning that takes place in our lives occurs when we are unconscious. Unconscious learning is *not knowing what you are learning* as well as *not knowing that you are in fact learning*. Learning begins at the onset of life and continues throughout life. Traditionally, learning is thought of as a conscious event with a source of information imparting knowledge that a person takes in. This form of learning is implied in the word, instruction.

Learning from experience is another form of learning that can take place in a less deliberate or conscious manner. Unconscious learning is the primary way we learn from experience in our love lives. In fact, unconscious learning is the very reason why most of us are not aware of what we've learned about love relationships. Since little if any instruction is given to us about love relationships, most of the learning we receive in this area occurs in this way. Furthermore, the absence of conscious intention and deliberation makes certain that what we learn unconsciously is subject to repetition and replication. You basically have no control over what you've learned if you've learned it unconsciously. Putting it all together, if you learn something unconsciously, healthy or unhealthy, and you have no control over it, you are bound to repeat what you've learned by recreating it over and over again.

As I indicated in the introduction of this book, what you've unconsciously learned is now in control.

Becoming conscious of what we've learned unconsciously is a necessary step in getting control over our love lives. The fact that a person could be recreating experiences in a relationship at odds with what he or she consciously wants is mind boggling to say the least. Just how unconscious learning takes control of your love life is still a bit mysterious. Are there parts of ourselves operating apart from and without the support of who we are and what we want? If true, this would guarantee a lot of internal conflict. For example, suppose I truly want to have a healthy love relationship, but I've unconsciously learned unhealthy lessons that result in the unconscious recreation of a lot of repetitive disappointment in my love life. *What I want would be at odds with what I've learned beyond my awareness.*

Learning How to Relate in Love

Now that we know, what we learn about love relationships is being used to determine the experience we have in our love lives, what do we learn about love relationships? The simple answer is *we learn how to relate in love.* Whether healthy or unhealthy, what we learn about love relationships determines how we relate when "in love." In love, of course, being a particular state of mind and body with its own unique characteristics. I'm sure you've encountered the idea of a difference between *loving someone* and *being in love with someone.* The former appears to be a more general description of affection, deep caring, love in the sense of having love for someone. Understandably, "love" as a general description of emotion or feeling has never been exclusively reserved for people. You can love a lot of things that aren't necessarily human (e.g. dog, cat, horse, job, vacation, money).

To be "in love with someone" is reserved exclusively for the experience of true love for a unique individual human being. In the state of "in love" there is an all-consuming quality to the emotion. It is special and deep, a unique state of emotion that is focused exclusively on one other human being. Perhaps that is the distinguishing element, the fact that unlike a more general sense of loving people, to be "in love" with someone is not substitutable.

There is also an implied longing to be with the person you are in love with. Love the emotion is known to be a uniting force, and in this case, it is most intensely a force to unite with this one particular individual. Our inherent need to love and be loved is most directly experienced in this particular state of mind and body.

Another interesting characteristic of this "in love" emotional state is that there appears to be an associated time warp. Past and present, in particular, are often merged in this state. Earlier I talked about how love life problems often involve the repetition and replication of past relationship experience. It appears that this exclusivity of focus on a particular individual and intensive emotional need in the "in love" state is its greatest strength and its greatest weakness.

Simply put, if your past love life experience, going all the way back to the beginning of your life, was positive and fulfilling, those relationship experiences will inevitably influence your current love life experiences in a positive way. However, if your earlier love life experiences were negative and toxic, the past influence on your current love life may be negative. A negative past experience of this kind influencing your current love life appears to be as tenacious in its repetition and replication as any positive experience would be. Negative influence from past experience being the single most deleterious influence on the health of our love lives.

What do we know so far? We now know that what we've learned about love relationships translates into an unconscious "blueprint" for how to relate in love. Whenever the "in love" emotional state occurs, without consciousness, we enter a state of mind and body that repeats and replicates a particular way of relating to the person we are now in love with. Furthermore, the success of this particular experience of being in love will depend upon how healthy the relationship is we have formed with the person we are in love with. If we form a healthy relationship, the love we feel is nurtured and grows. If we form an unhealthy relationship, the love we feel is deadened and dies.

Now it's time to get personal. To further dissect what you've learned about love relationships and how what you've learned determines the health of your specific love life, we'll have to go from the general "how to relate in love" to the specific "how do you relate in love?" What kind of love life experience are you, as an individual person, recreating in your particular love life? To go this deep, we are going to need to delve into the "psychology" of your unique love life and formulate a psychological concept to help us do so. In PART II of this book, I will introduce you to your *psychological love life*, the place in your mind that stores what you've learned about love relationships and determines what you'll recreate in your love life. Whether you know it or not.

PART II
PSYCHOLOGICAL
LOVE LIFE

CHAPTER 3

Your Psychological Love Life

⁓

Let's summarize what we know about the unhealthy love life. We know that a person with an unhealthy love life is either struggling with multiple disappointments or she has reached the stage of resignation, losing hope that she will ever have a healthy love relationship in her life. We know that the unhealthy love life is repetitive and tends to replicate a person's unhealthy relationship experiences in life. We also know that a person with an unhealthy love life recreates unhealthy relationship experiences by using what has been learned about love relationships.

Assuming that you've discovered that you have an unhealthy love life, what can be done about it? To change an unhealthy love life, you'll need to work on your **psychological love life**. Didn't think you had one? Well, we all have a psychological love life whether you consciously know it or not. Simply put, your psychological love life is the *internal mental representation* of what you've learned about love relationships that shapes the love life experiences you'll have going forward. To change your love life, you'll need to change your psychological love life.

We realized a while ago that true and permanent changes in a person's love life did not happen on the outside. Dressing differently, going to new places, acting differently can be helpful, but real change only occurs because a person changes what he has learned about love relationships. This simple truth has been shown to us over the years across many different love lives. What you've learned about love relationships is stored in your psychological love life, unconsciously and repetitively controlling your love life experiences, healthy or unhealthy.

What's in Your Psychological Love Life?

Your psychological love life has three parts: *your healthy or unhealthy relationship experiences, what was learned from those relationship experiences, and the aftereffects of unhealthy relationship experiences.* Your relationship experience is quite simply the experiences you have in the love relationships of your life starting from when you were born. They are stored in your psychological love life as emotional memory. Your relationship experiences in love are powerful learning experiences throughout your entire life. What you've learned from them is also stored in your psychological love life. Finally, when your relationship experiences in love are unhealthy, they create aftereffects which are encoded in your psychological love life as well. Let's talk about each part more extensively.

Unhealthy Relationship Experiences

The very first unhealthy relationship experience that came to my attention because it was showing up a lot in my clinical cases was "abuse." Many of my patients were repeating and replicating abuse in their adult love lives. It was not uncommon for a person needing treatment to talk about growing up in a domestically violent home and then marrying one or a series of domestically violent people. As if what was "familiar" was being unwittingly repeated and replicated in the person's adult love life. People were learning things about love relationships that they were recreating in their adult love relationships. I began to consider certain relationship experiences as "toxic" and influential in shaping the kind of adult love life experiences a person will have in life. In the case of relationship abuse, for example, it appeared that many people exposed to abuse earlier in life were learning how to abuse, be abused, or both in their adult love life, repeatedly in many instances.

I began to formulate a "list" of those relationship experiences that frequently appeared in the case material of patients who showed signs of an unhealthy love life. A sample of the unhealthy relationship experiences that would negatively influence how a person related in an adult love relationship. The following ten unhealthy relationship experiences were the most common:

Abandonment	Exploitation
Abuse	Mistrust
Control	Neglect
Dependency	Rejection
Dishonesty	Self-centeredness

Abandonment

This relationship experience is particularly virulent. It most commonly occurs as the result of the abandonment of a parent or other primary caregiver early in life. Abandonment involves a physically permanent separation from someone who is needed. The consequence is frequently a damaged view of attachment in adult interpersonal relationships. Interpersonal relationships are then chronically influenced by an expectation of loss.

The primary problem with abandonment is that the love related experiences that naturally occur as a consequence of a relationship are totally absent when a person is abandoned. For example, if you don't have a relationship with your father because he abandoned your family when you were young, identifications that would have taken place had he been present throughout your early life will be absent or incomplete. As an adult person, any efforts you make to heal the negative effects of abandonment, and build a renewed trust in attachment in your love life, would have to struggle against an enduring expectation of absence.

The difficulties some people have with commitment in a love relationship often have their origin in experiences of abandonment. People who have suffered abandonment earlier in their love lives tend to either find people who abandon them or they find people that they will abandon. In some instances, an individual both abandons and finds people who abandon alternately in the course of his or her love life as a consequence of abandonment earlier in life.

Common love life problems associated with an exposure to abandonment in life are: difficulty making and keeping commitments, making promises not kept, turbulent love relationships, avoiding love relationships out of fear of loss, painful separations, obsession with getting approval in love, and nervously trying to keep a love partner from leaving a love relationship while anticipating abandonment.

Abuse

Abuse, as I indicated earlier, was the first of these unhealthy relationship experiences to show its ugly influences in the love lives of our patients. Abuse represents one of the primary ways in which one person can hurt another in a love relationship. There are five different types of abuse according to our observations: *physical, sexual, emotional, verbal,* and *financial.* Physical, emotional, and verbal abuse being the most common. My son recounted an experience he had in a college class when the professor asked the class how many people were corporally punished growing up. Everyone (including the professor) raised their hands, except for my son. As we move toward a more conscious awareness of the violence that continues to pervade our society at all levels including child rearing, we may dispense with the rationalizations for it and realize that physical punishment is simply assault.

Sexual abuse is a frequent form of violence that can make its way into the adult love life. In most instances sexual abuse in the adult love life occurs in the form of sexual aggression without permission. The necessity for permission superseding the marital or relationship conventions two people can establish with each other. For example, rapes that occur in dating and marital relationships.

Emotional abuse involves abusing a person through the influence of toxic emotions. If I use guilt, anger, rage, fear, hate, etc. to affect you for some purpose, I am emotionally abusing you. Emotional abuse is sometimes a bit harder to detect due to the fact that emotions are being manipulated and the abuse is not always visible. Compare verbal abuse which involves noxious forms of verbal criticism and attack meant to deliberately hurt another. When abuse is verbal, it is often directed to another's weak points, vulnerabilities, or simply areas of doubt and worry. A deeper knowledge of another's sensitivities lends power to whatever verbal criticism is being levied against that person.

Finally, financial abuse involves an effort to obtain money from someone else, in many instances repeatedly and without concern for the state of the victim's resources. This type of abuse is commonly found in family, marital, or love relationships where dependency and/or envy are present. Financial abuse is frequently disguised as family obligations where there is an expectation of support even and most especially in instances where the abusing person has sufficient funds.

The adage "abuse begets abuse" is certainly true when this unhealthy relationship experience is perpetuated from generation to generation. Abuse teaches people how to abuse, how to be abused, or both, in their love lives. We found that the type of abuse being experienced early in life and the type of abuse that is recreated in a love life will often vary. For example, a person might grow up a victim of physical abuse in a family and recreate emotional abuse as an adult in a love relationship by emotionally abusing his or her partner. Or be verbally abused early in life and recreate the experience of being financially abused as an adult. Any combination of abuse in early life and the recreation of abuse in adulthood is possible. It's as if the experience of being "abused" itself rather than the type of abuse is what is communicated and perpetuated into adulthood.

Some common love life problems associated with an exposure to abuse in life are: sadomasochistic sexual relationships, domestic violence, verbal abuse in a love relationship, emotional abuse in a love relationship, financial abuse, tolerating disrespect in a love relationship, inability to stand up for oneself (i.e. setting limits on abuse), and rationalizing and excusing chronic mistreatment in a relationship.

Control

This form of unhealthy relationship experience occurs as a consequence of insecurity. Where the emotional security of one person depends upon the control of another. Control in a relationship can take the extreme form of overt control of another person's actions, possessiveness as an emotional and physical expression of ownership, and the expectation that another person should live according to one's own dictates and choices. In the extreme, overcontrol in a family or love relationship can constitute a form of domestic imprisonment. Keeping your spouse physically imprisoned in the family home would be an example of this. Prohibiting your partner from having relationships with her family or friends is another example.

Possessiveness, common in unhealthy love relationships, results in destructive jealousies, emotional insecurity, and control. The person you love belongs to you and no other. In its extreme form, the pathological jealousy possessiveness generates can generalize to just about anyone that comes in contact with the person you love. A milder form of control in a love relationship involves the use of expectation and approval to control the actions of another. Instead of overt actions tailored to control the person you love, the relationship itself is used to control your partner. A common example of a more subtle form of control would be the ways in which approvals and disapprovals are used to leverage the choices of another to keep them in line with what is expected.

Some people experience deep and disturbing insecurity when they fall in love. The vulnerability inherent in the experience of being in love is just too scary. The vulnerability they experience is the source of their insecurity. Suddenly someone else has become vital to one's own emotional security. For some people, this is intolerable. They think the only way to cope is to get control of the person they think is making them feel vulnerable. Over-control and possessiveness occur as a consequence of this insecurity in love relationships.

Some common love life problems associated with an exposure to excessive control in life are: authoritarian relationships, possessiveness, domestic imprisonment, inability to separate from one's family of origin while in a committed or marital relationship, insecurity in a love relationship, intrusive in-laws and/or family members, physical and/or psychological domination in a love relationship, and rigid self-control.

Dependency

Dependency is an unhealthy relationship experience when a person is dependent upon another for what she or he can provide for herself or himself. This form of dependency is experienced as neediness and will engender guilt feelings if not adequately responded to. There is often an air of childishness about the dependent person. His "needs" are often childish and constitute efforts to procure a "parental response" from other adults regardless of the dependent person's age. Ultimately, unhealthy dependency needs can never be satisfied. In fact, this is yet another way in which dependency, as an expression of unhealthy relationship experience, differs from the normal dependency of children or elderly persons who are no longer capable of caring for themselves.

Dependent people are experienced as needy in a love relationship. They fear separations and are usually worried about losing someone. In a love relationship they are usually focused on what they can get from their love partner. What is less important is what they can give to their partners and ultimately to themselves. Dependent people in love operate under the limited notion that everything they need in life will come from somebody else. This perspective on love reinforces the feeling other people will inevitably have that they are a burden.

Some common love life problems associated with an exposure to dependency in life are: clinging and neediness in a love relationship, difficulty separating from family of origin enough to have a healthy love relationship, lack of independence in a love relationship, being a self-sacrificing caregiver in love relationships, viewing love partners as unable to take care of themselves, and trying to repeatedly rescue or fix the person you fall in love with.

Dishonesty

Lies are a corrosive force in a love relationship. Lying eventually destroys love precisely because you are unable to "locate" the person you are in love with. When the person you love lies, at whatever frequency, you are no longer able to judge with confidence the presence of that person in your life. Who is she? Where is he? What is she? These questions become impossible to answer with certainty.

If lies are by "commission," the meaning of facts are distorted in favor of a certain outcome and impact on another person. If lies are by "omission," facts are omitted for the concealed purpose of once again having a certain impact on another person. The problem with lying is, like with potato chips, "it's impossible to eat just one." The practice is addictive, to say the least. Consider the temptation. Let's say the first lie accomplishes the feat of misrepresenting something to someone, and you get off Scott free. The power of that simple little act is immense. Like a credit card, can you limit it to simply one purchase? Most liars like gamblers and addicts, are convinced they can indulge and stay in control. This is by design impossible. A false life eventually and predictably falls apart.

The love life problem that is most commonly associated with dishonesty is cheating or infidelity. Plain and simple, when you cheat you are lying. Liars in love usually try to live double, triple or quadruple lives. One persona for one person, another for another, and so on. They simply don't believe in the idea of a "true self." Keeping all the lies in order and separate is stressful to say the least. Most liars in love don't or won't acknowledge that. One of the biggest problems with this kind of love life is the limited intimacy. If you are lying, you are not really known by the person you are lying to. Furthermore, a love life with more than one person in it, when you are committed to just one of them and lying to him or her, is another reason the intimacy you'll have will be limited. True emotional intimacy will always be measured in terms of the depth of love you experience with the particular person you are in love with.

Some common love life problems associated with an exposure to dishonesty in life are: cheating in a love relationship with multiple partners, manipulating love partners, presenting a false self in relationship, compulsive lying by omission and commission in a love relationship, repeatedly being cheated on in love relationships, gullibility in relationships (i.e. believing lies even when the truth is known), poor judgment in love.

Exploitation

When you've been exposed to the unhealthy relationship experience of exploitation, you've been sized up and played. A genuine healthy love relationship has been replaced by utility disguised by make-believe. The more subtle the exploitation, the more intricate the make-believe relationship. Now people serve a "purpose" and we are no longer talking about love relationships. It's a matter of getting benefits. You no longer care about who another person is. It becomes exclusively what he or she can do for you. This reduction of human experiencing to utilitarian relatedness, risks a form of social depersonalization that turns people into things. The philosopher Martin Buber warned us against this type of objectification of people (1958).

The love life problem most frequently associated with the unhealthy relationship experience of being exploited is learning to tolerate being used and getting very little back. When you are exposed to a steady diet of exploitation in your life, chances are you'll get used to this inequity, ignoring it, especially when it shows up in a love relationship. You could be the type of exploited person who runs around and does all kinds of things for everybody else, not asking for or *visibly* needing anything for yourself. I said visibly because what's on the surface is never the whole story. Unfortunately, there are too many people out there who will intuit the fact that you're willing to overlook this imbalance in a love relationship and sacrifice yourself. This one-way exploitation tends to regenerate itself in an exploited person's love life.

Some common love life problems associated with an exposure to exploitation early in life are: predatory relationships with love partners, treating potential partners like "objects" to be used, being used financially, sexually, or emotionally in a love relationship, being oblivious to exploitation in a relationship, and various forms of self-abnegation.

Mistrust

This unhealthy relationship experience involves an exposure to a love relationship that discourages the experience of trust. Whether early or later in life, and without justification, you are not considered trustworthy. The outcome of this kind of mistreatment early in life is usually a damaged or underdeveloped ability to trust or be trusted. Without the reliable ability to trust or be trusted, a healthy love life is virtually impossible.

Mistrusting relationships are usually distant and defensive in nature. For the most part, mistrust in love relationships is focused on the possibility of and protection from "hurt." This type of unhealthy relationship experience will most likely be carried into the adult love life in the form of mistrust that another person will not be able to take proper care of your heart. It's easy to come to the unfortunate conclusion that it's probably better if you just take care of yourself instead.

In a love relationship, a mistrusting person will probably keep the person he or she loves at a distance. The expectation in love is that people are not to be trusted. Even the ones you get to know. I find that current suspicions are usually generated from past experiences of hurt that have not been resolved. Resolved in the sense that a renewed faith in your ability to take the risk of being in love has been recreated. Notice I said "recreated," because you were born with the ability to trust intact, a gift from Mother Nature to be sure.

If you grow up with mistrusting people and you haven't done a damn thing to deserve that mistrust, the constant exposure to suspicion will take its toll. I've heard of so many instances over the years where expectations were so powerful that they influenced people to create the very thing being suspected. A patient once said to me, "My wife was so adamant that I was cheating on her, and I wasn't, but she accused me of it so many times, out of frustration and anger I cheated on her. There you go, happy now? I've confirmed your suspicion and subsequent mistrust for you." Self-fulfilling prophesy, or should I say fulfilling a prophesy for someone else?

Some common love life problems associated with an exposure to mistrust in life are: suspiciousness of people in your love partner's life, difficulty trusting the person you love, difficulty communicating feelings openly in a love relationship, being a secretive person in love who is difficult to get to know, being chronically jealous in love, and chronic self-doubts in love.

Neglect

Neglect as an unhealthy relationship experience involves exposure to "part-time caring" while growing up or even in adult love relationships. Neglect can be physical and/or emotional. Someone once told me that she preferred abandonment to neglect. In her view, abandonment is excruciatingly painful but because the offending person goes away, there is a chance to heal. On the other hand, neglect repetitively inflicts the pain of loss, and the victim never has a chance to heal.

Neglect in a love relationship engenders a false hope. A hope that the love desired and needed will be forthcoming. A hope that keeps you looking for an opportunity to finally get what you've longed for. In that hopeful state of mind and emotional need, disappointment is repetitive. This cycle of hope and disappointment is extremely difficult to get out of. Imagine a young child being brought up by a mother whose ambivalence toward the child is expressed as an inconsistency in caring for the child's emotional needs. The child is focused exclusively on obtaining the needed love and attention from the parent, ostensibly because you only have one mother or father, and that mother or father *should love you*. What does it take for that child to realize that the neglect received is an ongoing feature of this particular mother's character or parenting ability?

The potential for neglect in a love relationship to teach neglectful behavior in love to offspring is exceedingly high. The lessons can occur in the form of finding someone who is neglectful, or neglecting someone you find, or both in the same love life. Neglectful love relationships early in life teach people to unconsciously expect that something will be lacking in a love relationship.

A common form of this kind of love life problem is the "triangle" love life. In the triangle love life, a person falls in love with someone who is not emotionally available. This could be someone else's wife, husband, girlfriend, or boyfriend. Falling in love with a committed person guarantees the feeling of being neglected and deprived of something you need. And commitments are not just limited to other people. Falling in love with a person who is committed to work, to travel, to some activity, to a substance, or to a group that limits his or her *emotional availability* is the factor that recreates the neglect.

Some common love life problems associated with an exposure to neglect in life are: pattern of giving sparsely in a love relationship, depriving the person you love of attention, affection or caring, falling in love with a person who is committed to another (e.g. married person), getting into and staying in "triangles" too long, disallowing one's emotional needs in a love relationship, not knowing how to take care of oneself in a love relationship,

Rejection

Rejection as an unhealthy relationship experience in love involves exposure to the idea and feeling that there is something wrong with you. The way that you are, yourself, your presence, is simply unacceptable. To be rejected in this way, especially during the vulnerable years in your life, is devastating for your self-esteem. Self-esteem is predicated on the belief that you are acceptable and lovable.

Inevitably there is a sensitive time in life when you will be reliant on the judgement and opinion of others. In many instances, this reliance makes its way well into adulthood, but for this example let's focus on childhood and adolescence. Psychologists have found that psychological maturation involves a period in life when identifying with adults is a preamble to becoming your own person (Mahler, 1968; Mahler et al., 1975). If what you are exposed to is rejection growing up, inevitably rejection will become part of the way you relate to yourself and others. There are more than enough unfortunate painful examples of rejection teaching rejection in adulthood love relationships.

People exposed to rejection as an unhealthy relationship experience growing up, or in adulthood, tend to find people who reject them, or people they reject or both. Adult rejection commonly occurs in the form of verbal criticism and negative judgement. A person who has been rejected, for example as a child, will struggle with lower than adequate levels of self-esteem and the complications this can bring to a love relationship. Needing someone you're in love with to approve of you, can be a burden imposed on a love relationship. Of course, the added problem is, no matter how much approval you get, it will never be enough.

Some common love life problems associated with an exposure to rejection in life are: chronic criticism of the person you love, excessive judgmentalism in love, perfectionism, low self-confidence in a love relationship, poor self-esteem in love, difficulty initiating sex or an emotional connection with the person you love, and severe self-criticalness in love.

Self-centeredness

In this contemporary age, self-centeredness abounds. It appears that the jump from narcissism to genuine loving is getting harder instead of easier. The distractions and complications are multiplying. Growing up in the midst of self-centered relationships involves exposure to a social environment that is in essence, not intimate. Intimacy implies that people are sharing of themselves with each other, and getting to know each other as a consequence. In a self-centered relationship, you simply don't learn intimacy. Instead self-centeredness begets more self-centeredness and/or feelings of insignificance.

In a self-centered relationship there is figuratively only one person in the relationship. Although the word relationship implies an interaction between two entities or more, let's assume that the self-centered person is relating to himself. Any other person in the relationship is relegated to the role of attending to the self-centered person. How is it possible to relate to someone who believes, acts, and feels it is all about him? Answer, without much of a self. Unfortunately, there are plenty of people in the world who have learned how to annex themselves to a self-centered person in this way. By my calculations, they learned it growing up with self-centered people and have found a way to repeat and replicate the same limited adaptation over and over again in adulthood. This is all too common in adult love relationships.

If you've been exposed to a good dose of self-centeredness on the part of other people growing up, you've probably learned how to "audience." By this I mean, provide the self-centered person with the attention he or she craves. Of course, along with this skill will be the lesson of "insignificance." Self-centered people are notorious for making their audience feel ultimately insignificant. If you fall in love with a self-centered person, expect to be in the audience and feeling insignificant at one point or another. The problem for the self-centered adult in love is the fact that many people outgrow the insignificance I'm talking about. This can result in a feeling of emotional injury if the self-centered person's partner is one of them. Self-centered people suffer when they are not the center of attention.

Some common love life problems associated with an exposure to self-centeredness in life are: difficulty empathizing with your love partner's emotional pain, devaluing the person you love, not knowing what and when to feel in love, staying in a relationship with the feeling of insignificance too long, not knowing how to ask for what you need, chronic shyness in love, passive-aggressiveness in a love relationship, and falling in love with people you adore in a self-sacrificing manner.

Learned Beliefs, Behavior, and Feelings

How is learning about love relationships used to recreate how you relate in love? Recreating familiar relationship experience requires the combined effects of what is unconsciously *believed* about love relationships, what *actions* are taken in a love relationship, and what *feelings* are generated by those beliefs and behavior in a love relationship. Beliefs, behavior and feelings constitute the raw materials required to recreate familiar relationship experience in your love life. Of course, remember none of this is done consciously and is the net result of what is learned about love relationships as a consequence of exposure to healthy or unhealthy relationship experience.

Belief + Behavior → Feeling

Our Learning Formula: Belief + Behavior → Feeling predicts that what we "believe" about love relationships and how we "act" in a love relationship will generate how we "feel" in a love relationship. Staying with our current focus on the recreation of unhealthy relationship experience, let's elaborate a bit on each of the elements in this formula.

What you believe about love relationships will shape the kind of experiences you'll have in your love relationship. How so? Does it seem odd to you that a belief could be powerful enough to determine the kind of experience you'll have in your life? Many people might disagree with this notion and assume that belief has little or no power to determine experience. Yet there are plenty of examples in everyday life to the contrary.

A simple example might be the experience of getting bad news. You are feeling good and it's an optimistic day. Unfortunately, you receive bad news from someone you trust, informing you that something tragic has happened to someone or something you care about. The end result is usually some form of mental and physical anguish. That mental and physical anguish was created by a belief, nothing more. A belief in the validity of the news you were given. If you didn't believe what you were told, let's say because you didn't trust the messenger, no anguish. It's your belief in the truth of what you've been told that creates your emotional and physical pain.

You grow up in a family and for one reason or another you are neglected. Your emotional needs as a child and adolescent were not properly cared for with any degree of consistency. The years you've spent coping with and tolerating this inadequate care have convinced you that love relationships are inherently neglectful. In reality, you only have your family relationship experiences to draw from to come to this conclusion. We can say, your unhealthy relationship experience in your early life (i.e. neglect) has unconsciously taught you to *believe* that love relationships are neglectful. Now you might know superficially that logically and rationally there are people in the world who are not neglectful, and you may even have met a few. But deep down inside, because of your particular experience, learned at a time of considerable vulnerability while needing love from family members, you'll believe neglect always accompanies love.

What you believe about love relationships is complemented by *what you do in a love relationship.* Your exposure to certain unhealthy relationship experiences will unknowingly teach you how to act in a love relationship. Our research in this area showed us that people tend to recreate unhealthy relationship experiences in their love lives in one of three ways: *by doing to another what was done to you, by getting another to do what was done to you to you, or both.* Let's elaborate.

Doing to another what was done to you involves looking for and finding a person with whom you can "actively" recreate your unhealthy relationship experience. If I was abused in the love relationships of my early life, I could unknowingly recreate this unhealthy relationship experience by looking for and finding someone to abuse "in love." My unconscious preference would be to actively recreate the unhealthy relationship experience I experienced with someone who is receptive to this because of his or her own experiences. It's amazing how many people, taught by abuse to abuse, find people who gravitate toward relationships of abuse. This is unfortunately true of any and all of the unhealthy relationship experiences I've listed earlier.

One technical point worth making is that sometimes, and I'm not sure about the frequency of this phenomenon, looking for someone to enact an unhealthy relationship experience can result in a "mismatch." What I mean is, you might unconsciously assume that the person you've found is a good complement to whatever relationship experience you are recreating, however in reality he or she is not. In situations like this it is common for the love relationship to have conflict and end sooner than later. For example, if you marry a person you assume is going to "accept" the self-centeredness you've learned growing up in self-centered family relationships, there is a possibility that you may have misperceived her compatibility. My guess is this kind of situation occurs, at least some of the time, because the intensity of what is learned from unhealthy relationship experience can be strong enough to obscure and distort our perception of another.

Then there are people who are exposed to unhealthy relationship experiences and prefer to, again unknowingly, seek out people who will do to him or her what was done to him or her in the past. In this instance, your unhealthy relationship experience is recreated by finding someone to mistreat you in the way you were mistreated in love. The victims of this particular way of recreating unhealthy relationship experiences in love are quite common in a clinical practice. Probably because people victimized in this way are often honest enough with themselves to recognize the problem, at least on the surface, and seek treatment for it. We've had plenty of success bringing this kind of recreation into consciousness and helping people change it.

Lastly, there is the hybrid formation where you alternate between one and the other recreation during the course of your love life. This involves alternating between doing to your love partner what was done to you, then getting your love partner to do to you what was done to you, either in a single love relationship or across several. Do you see the differences?

Do we know why some people prefer enacting what was done to them to someone else versus finding others to do it to them? Not really. Maybe it's personality, or some other personal circumstance that generates one preference over another. It doesn't seem like choice, at least not the conscious variety of choice.

I tend to attribute this preference to the personal experience of learning that takes place when this kind of unhealthy relationship experience is being taught. For example, if you're a small child and witness the rejection of one family member by another, you might "identify" more closely with the rejecting person because of the emotional pain you see in the victim. Your preference is then based on an avoidance reaction that naturally occurs. Alternately, you could be more emotionally attached to the victim in such a family scenario resulting in a greater empathic connection to him or her and the later recreation of the victim's perceived experience in your own love life. In this instance, your preference would be largely based on identification.

Then of course you have the generated feelings that occur as a consequence of what you believe and how you behave in a love relationship. Let's start this part of our discussion by differentiating between "emotions" and "feelings," two terms that are frequently used interchangeably. For our purposes, *emotions* are natural, biologically derived, innate experiences that are built into our mind-body. We are instinctively constructed to experience them unpredictably and uncontrollably. The controversy, however, is focused on which affective experiences we would include to form a complete list of natural emotions that everybody can agree on. Putting that to the side, I'll make the case that *love* and *grief* are most certainly on the list of natural emotions.

On the other hand, *feelings* are a *learned* phenomenon. I believe feelings are generated from what we believe and how we behave. What we believe about love relationships and how we behave in love generates certain feelings. These generated feelings are the predictable outcome of the unhealthy relationship experiences that have taught us certain beliefs and behaviors about love relationships.

In the case of unhealthy relationship experience, the feelings being generated are "toxic." Toxic in the sense of contaminating with negative feelings the experience of love in a love relationship. The various feelings being generated from whatever unhealthy relationship experiences have taught you get mixed with the emotion of love in a love relationship. If I was unwittingly taught to believe that love relationships are inherently dishonest because of the dishonesty I endured or witnessed coming up in the world, chances are my love relationships would recreate dishonesty and generate the feeling that someone is being deceived in those relationships.

Abandonment: **Loss**	Exploitation: **Used**
Abuse: **Fearful**	Mistrust: **Suspicious**
Control: **Trapped**	Neglect: **Deprived**
Dependency: **Needy**	Rejection: **Rejected**
Dishonesty: **Deceived**	Self-centeredness: **Insignificant**

Our list of ten unhealthy relationship experiences can now be presented with the feelings they generate in the adult love life. As I indicated earlier, these generated feelings contaminate the experience of love, the natural unpredictable emotion we human beings can experience from time to time. Remember, the word relationship in the phrase "love relationship" is the product of how you've learned to relate in a love relationship. How you "feel" about a love relationship is an important part of what you've learned. If the feeling is negative or unhealthy, it will interfere with and limit the love you experience. For example, feeling "trapped" in a love relationship because you've learned from the unhealthy relationship experience of being over-controlled to expect too much control in a love relationship will predictably interfere with the experience of love in your relationship.

Aftereffects of What You've Experienced

Aftereffects can occur in your psychological love life if the relationship experiences you were exposed to in your life were hurtful. In the case of unhealthy relationship experiences, there are variable degrees of emotional pain associated with each experience. Aftereffects are basically the ways in which you try to cope with, fix, and ultimately protect yourself from being hurt again in your love life. They are basically the defenses you can use to avoid further emotional pain. The disadvantage is that aftereffects can rigidify an unhealthy love life and interfere with efforts to make improvements. We'll get back to that later in this discussion.

Let's start with a brief exploration of the nature of *hurt* in a love life. Imagine two types of love life hurt, *intentional hurt* and *unintentional hurt*. Intentional hurt involves a premeditated conscious effort to hurt someone you are in a love relationship with. Basically, you would be trying to hurt, for whatever reason, the person you love. This kind of hurt is fundamentally antithetical to healthy love relations. It's an ingredient of many unhealthy relationship experiences and the worst part is that it's intentional. If you are in a relationship with someone who is intentionally hurting you, most likely it's toxic and time to leave.

Unintentional hurt, on the other hand, is an inevitable part of a healthy love relationship. Despite all the idealized notions you might have about true love being beyond hurt, realistically, you can't be in love without feeling unintentional hurt from time to time. I remember my beloved analyst, after listening to me drone on about how anxious I felt moving my fiancé into my bachelor pad because now she could hurt me, asked me where I had gotten the idea that I could be in love without ever getting hurt. I can remember how unsettling that question was. You mean I don't have absolute control over whether or not I'll be hurt in this marriage I am planning to have? You see, aftereffects are often the result of this kind of unrealistic belief that you can avoid unintentional hurt in your love relationship.

How does unintentional hurt occur? If there are two people in a love relationship, which there usually are, you will inevitably experience *differences*. Differences mean disagreements, different perspectives, different opinions, etc. For two unique individuals in love, no matter how much mutual interest or common ground there is, differences are inevitable. The way I personally integrated this understanding into my philosophy about love relationships was to assume that differences are easier to work with if I believe in and trust my natural ability to heal the unintentional hurts of love. In fact, the risk of "falling in love" as an unpredictable and out of control experience of loving and needing another human being, is made much more tolerable by believing in one's natural ability to heal. If hurt did lead to loss, you'd be able to grieve, heal your heart, and move on in your love life. Let's talk about the two most common aftereffects that people employ when trying to cope with and protect themselves from the hurts of an unhealthy love life.

Changing Partners Instead of Yourself

Changing partners has two implicit meanings. The first is to actually change the person you are in a love relationship with. For example, you have changed partners (from one person to another) frequently in your love life. The second meaning is you try to change the one person you are in a love relationship with. I mean really try to change him or her to conform to whatever you believe is right for you and him or her in the relationship. Let's talk about the aftereffect of changing partners from one to another first.

Remember that aftereffects in your psychological love life, your internal mental love life, occur because of some unhealthy relationship experience you've endured. You are now trying to cope with the possibility of being hurt again and again in your adult love life. Changing partners, as you look for someone better than the last person you found, reduces your chances of getting hurt again. Deeper intimacy with one person over time is always associated with more vulnerability to hurt. Remember the 20th century "playboy?" He was immune to hurt because he never stayed long enough with one person to experience the depth required to be "in love." At the time that particular way of life was romanticized. But for someone in my profession, this implicit avoidance of intimacy means the playboy was doing his best to avoid recreating some kind of experience of hurt. I think the phrase we used to throw around was "fear of intimacy." Serial love relationships that are kept limited in depth, involving substitutable partners, are considered in this research to be a form of aftereffect derived from an unwitting exposure to unhealthy relationship experiences in life.

Then of course we have the equally common effort to actually change one's love partner as the other variation on this aftereffect. Trying to change someone usually exists on a continuum from *force*, to *manipulation*, to *fixing or rescuing*, to garden variety *expectations* that your love partner should conform to what you believe is good for him and you. Force being the more aggressive form of trying to change someone, and expectation being the more subtle form. By the way, I'm using the phrase "trying to change someone" because it's impossible to accomplish. You'll only get resistance and resentment.

People change themselves, anything else is not real change. This necessitates an understanding that in love if you are not getting what you want, the best course of action is to leave and find what you need somewhere else. Trying to change him or her is guaranteed to be a great waste of time. A friend once told me that the key to a healthy love life is to find someone whose faults you can live with. Nevertheless, many people continue to try changing the person they love.

Remember Mr. and Mrs. Potato-head? The different colorful parts of the head are interchangeable. Depending on your mood, you could change the eyes, nose, ears, mouth, etc. Trying to change your partner is kind of like playing with Mr. or Mrs. Potato-head. You are trying to make the person you love into what you might need him or her to be rather than who he or she already is. Another way to illustrate this impossible venture is to think of a love relationship as building a robot. When you're building a robot, you aren't really focused on who the person you love already is or isn't. You are focused on who you want the person to become, in the case of a robot, from scratch. To build a robotic person, you'll already have the physical and functional aspects of the robot clearly in mind. For those of us who know the impossible task of trying to change someone into someone else, it's much easier to build a robot.

One last comment about changing a person in love. The only person you can change is yourself, we've already established that. Taken a step further, the only true way to really and permanently change your love life is to change yourself. We'll be exploring a very effective method of changing your love life by changing yourself in the next part of this book. For now, I would like to emphasize again the importance of this counter-intuitive method of changing your love life. Most people think about changing their love lives by making changes on the outside first and foremost. Pick a different person, wear a different suit or dress, a different hairdo, a better dating app, a better restaurant, a more attractive way of acting in public, none of these really work. You'll have to change something in your psychological love life to achieve permanent improvement in your love life.

Defensiveness to Avoid Vulnerability

The other prominent aftereffect that is commonly included in your psychological love life involves an outright defensiveness to avoid vulnerability in love. There are three general types of love life defense: *avoidance*, *distance*, and *conflict*. All three are ways of stopping the possibility of hurt in your love life. Under each type there are an endless number of things that can be used to accomplish defensive avoidance, distance, and conflict. Examples of each category would be: you can avoid a love relationship and cut down on the possibility of hurting yourself in one by not going to places where you might meet eligible love partners; you can maintain distance in your love relationship by limiting the amount of communication you have with the person you live with in a love relationship; or you can use conflict to protect yourself against vulnerability in love by being critical of your mate every time an opportunity for intimacy presents itself. As I said, there are endless variations in our creative ability to construct defenses against the potential hurts of being in love.

Of course, defensiveness in love has its limitations and disadvantages. For one, when you're chronically defensive in a love relationship you are interfering with your own ability to give and receive love in the relationship. And unfortunately, your defenses in love, especially if you are not aware of them, can become chronic. What this means is you'll tend to rely on particular ways of defending yourself, and you'll keep relying on them with little change over the course of your love life. Becoming aware of how you are defending yourself against hurt in love is no small matter. It'll usually involves some form of discomfort to say the least. What you are ultimately trying to achieve using defenses in your love life is a love relationship without the experience of vulnerability. Sorry, it's just not possible.

Let's talk about vulnerability in love, so I can make this a bit clearer. Since love, the emotion, is unpredictable and uncontrollable, it's going to be an experience you "fall into." This is precisely why we use the phrase "falling in love." The connotation here is that you've lost control. Love is a spontaneous emotional experience that happens to you, you don't make it happen. Remember the only thing we can control in a love relationship is the way we relate in love. This being the case, vulnerability as an experience in love is inevitable. Of course, you can block vulnerability with defenses. You can even put it off hoping for a time when you'll feel like you are more in control.

At some point however, you may realize as many people do in love, that vulnerability is the emotional experience that indicates you are *open* to giving and receiving love. Vulnerability makes this so. As a psychologist, it's not easy trying to convince people of this. Most people in love, at some point or another, try to be in love defensively. By the way, the rewards you'll get for tolerating vulnerability in your love relationship are the easier time you'll have healing the unintentional hurts you'll inevitably experience, and of course, the love you'll give and get for doing so.

PART III
UNLEARNING METHOD

CHAPTER 4

Changing Your Psychological Love Life

Unlearning Formula

Earlier we talked about learning unconsciously from experience in your love life. Just like you have developed your ability to learn, you can develop your ability to *unlearn*. Unlearning in this context means, you will have the option to undo the learning you've done without awareness in your love relationships starting from the moment of your birth. More specifically, what you've learned from experience that is *unhealthy.* In the case of your love life, most if not all of what you've learned was unconscious. You didn't really know that it was happening. To begin this undoing process, I am calling unlearning, your first and most important step is to *become aware of what you've learned.*

The next step in this unlearning process is to use your newly achieved consciousness to select what you want to unlearn. For the purpose of improving your love life, the primary interest of this book, you will probably want to choose what was unhealthy to be unlearned. Unhealthy learning in your love life is the consequence of being exposed to unhealthy relationship experiences. Even though some of the unhealthy relationship experiences we can be exposed to never make it into the way you've learned how to relate in love, some will. You'll become conscious of what you've learned that is unhealthy, then you'll select the unhealthy learning that has gotten into your love life for unlearning.

How what we've learned about love relationships gets unlearned is an interesting process. Once conscious, you have the ability to apply your consciousness in the form of a therapeutic self-critique. The purpose being to *disrupt* the psychological hold what you've learned has over your love life experience. Remember, your psychological love life is your internal love life template, if you will, that determines the form your love life experience is going to take. When you've consciously identified what you've learned that is unhealthy and interferes with forming a healthy love relationship, you now have to *challenge* its dominance in your mind.

What we unconsciously learn about love relationships prefers to operate silently behind the scenes controlling and shaping the kinds of love life experiences we are going to have in our love lives. Problem is, when what we've learned is unhealthy, our love life experience will be repetitively unhealthy. The good news is, we human beings have the innate ability to oppose a part of our minds with another part of our minds. This state of internal conflict in this kind of unlearning situation is fundamentally therapeutic. It's a stage in the process of changing your mind and behavior.

For example, suppose you believe something that is not healthy and has caused you problems in your life. It's something you started believing without much consciousness and you've held onto the belief for a while. For some reason you become aware of how unhealthy your belief is. This awareness will be at odds with what you believe for a time. Until your awareness of how unhealthy your belief is, becomes stronger, and you are able to disrupt and challenge the actions your unhealthy belief generates and controls. At some point, your awareness of a better healthier belief will take hold because it has strengthened to the point where it can oppose and relinquish the dominance of the unhealthy belief. This is the process of mental change. The consciousness you've created to challenge and disrupt the unhealthy learning you've formed, because of the unhealthy relationship experiences you've been subjected to, will go through a similar unlearning process. When you change your mind, you go from awareness of what you've learned to unlearning.

Let's add a third step to this unlearning to complete the process. You'll go from becoming aware of a problem, to challenging and disrupting its grip on your experiences, to *learning or relearning something healthier*. Learning something new that is better, or relearning something old that was better, learned in the past, and forgotten. Challenging and disrupting unhealthy love life learning is like throwing away old furniture that no longer looks good and is uncomfortable to use. Once the old furniture is gone, you can move some new stuff in. Naturally, you first have to get rid of the old furniture before there is "room" to bring something better into your home.

Newly learned or relearned experience is the "corrective" for unhealthy learning. A simple but potent way of thinking about this is to assume that the corrective for whatever you've learned from your unhealthy relationship experiences would be the *opposite* of what you've learned. A simple example would be, if you've grown up in an abusive family that taught you that love relationships are "abusive," a relationship experience in the present that is "respectful" would be therapeutic. Respectful relationship experience being the opposite of abusive relationship experience. Consciously looking for and sustaining a respectful love relationship would be the way to effectively work on your love life.

However, this last addition to the unlearning process requires practice. Why? It appears that what you've learned, which you are trying to unlearn, doesn't go away so easily. Even though changes are made, temptations to return to what you've learned earlier in your life will tend to reoccur. Perhaps a better way to understand this unlearning process is to view the change from what you've learned to unlearning as requiring repeated reinforcement. Old learning can be stubborn. If you've learned to be dishonest in love because you grew up observing people in love tell each other lies, even after realizing the importance of the truth in love, your tendency to consider lying will continue to exist in your mind. Reaffirming change becomes a practice to make sure that change endures over time. In effect, to sustain healthy change, we are forever keeping the new, current -- and the old, in the past.

Now you've become conscious of what you've learned about love relationships, challenged what was unhealthy, and replaced what was unhealthy with opposite healthy experience and learning. The unlearning process is now complete.

In summary, this unlearning process has evolved into the following *unlearning formula:*

Learned → Unlearn → Learn or Re-learn

What was learned about love relationships can be unlearned and something healthier learned or re-learned. This unlearning formula was originally developed by the educational psychologist, John Dewey (Lamons, 2012), and told to me by the psychoanalyst, Benjamin Wolstein (personal communication), who studied with Dewey at Columbia University. This unlearning formula is an important part of Dewey's perspective on experiential learning and Wolstein's empirical theory and practice of interpersonal psychoanalysis (Wolstein, 1964, 1976, 1971). It has proved to be invaluable as a way to understand how we learn in our love lives and how what we learn can be changed. The three steps of our Unlearning Method are derived from this unlearning formula.

Who Taught You About Love Relationships?

Before applying our Unlearning Method for making permanent changes in how you relate in your love relationships, an important prerequisite must occur. You have to know *who the person or persons were that taught you about love relationships.* Once you've become conscious of the fact that someone (or more than one person) in your life has had a powerful influence on what you believe about love relationships, how you behave in love relationships, and how you feel about love relationships, the answer to the question, who taught you, usually comes pretty quickly. Not everyone in your life gets to teach you about love relationships.

I find that usually, the source of experience and learning will be quite specific and sometimes surprising. For example, you could have been exposed to several of my listed unhealthy relationship experiences, let's say, control, dishonesty, and neglect. Yet only control and neglect have found their way into your love life. Not sure why some people are affected by a particular unhealthy relationship experience and others are not. It's probably the complicated consequence of being uniquely different individuals, with unique personalities, and uniquely different experiences in life.

"Who taught you" always comes before "what you were taught." As I alluded to earlier, I believe on some subliminal level, we all know who has gotten into our love lives even if we haven't admitted it to ourselves or anybody else. And the usual differences between people don't really matter. Like the gender of the person who influenced you, or even the amount of presence he or she had in your life. I've heard of people being influenced by someone, a father or mother, he or she rarely if ever saw, only heard about from other family members. Identifying "who taught you about love relationships" allows you to then figure out "what unhealthy relationship experiences" were taught and from there the remaining contents of your psychological love life.

In our love life research, the extent to which we "internalize" other people's love lives is astounding. By internalize I mean bring their love life experience as an influence into your own psychological love life. I think there are a couple of ways to do that. On a conscious more deliberate level, you could "imitate" the love life of someone you look up to in your life. Maybe because you believe the particular person had a love life worth admiring. If the internalization of someone else's love life is done unconsciously you'll identify with the person. Identification means you've internalized someone else's love life without necessarily knowing you have, and there is a good possibility it won't be derived from admiration. We can identify with a person just because we live with him or her. It's another way of describing the unconscious learning experience I mentioned earlier.

Here's the problem with identifying with another person's love life. It's not yours! Your love life should be uniquely your own. It should belong to you, exclusively, and no one else. When your love life belongs to you it is vastly more satisfying. Think of it, a love life built from your own thoughts, feelings, choices, desires, wants, etc. Not because someone else shows you what he or she did, or even tells you what he or she did and urges, directs, assumes you'll do the same. A common love life problem in my private practice has been curing the unhappiness or dissatisfaction that inevitably occurs when a person imitates or identifies with someone else's love life.

I have worked with people who married someone their mothers wanted them to marry. For whatever reason, and the reason was usually not love, perhaps a mother felt a particular person was her daughter's (or son's) ideal partner. At some point in middle age, let's say 30s to 50s, the influence of a mother's love life choice tends to wane, and the son or daughter's truer feeling about the chosen partner comes to the surface. This emergent experience of true feeling about someone you were directed to marry is often the reason why many marriages fail in middle-age.

What happens psychologically when you've identified the person or persons responsible for teaching you about love relationships? You now have an opportunity to *individuate,* or make personal your love life experience. How is this done? Once you've become aware that your love life experience is being determined by someone else's influence, you can begin to *separate* yourself and *differentiate* yourself from that influence. It's akin to taking control of your love life, precisely what our Unlearning Method was designed to help you do. You'll know you are in control of your love life, again or for the very first time, when it's your *choices* that determine your love life experiences not someone else's experiences or opinions.

Unlearning Method

If you're serious about needing to improve your love life, really improve it, you'll take the "tools" described in the following section, outlined in a simple how to format, and apply them to your love life. Your goal is to become aware of the unhealthy relationship experiences that have gotten into your love life, challenge their uncontrolled influence on your love relationships, and find the specific type of relationship experience that will "correct" the negative effects of the unhealthy relationship experiences you were exposed to.

This chapter describes our Unlearning Method in a simple step-by-step instruction for anyone interested in making the needed changes in their love life on their own.

How to Apply the Unlearning Method

Step 1 - Identify Your Psychological Love Life

Remember, everyone has a *psychological love life*, the "blueprint" you unwittingly keep in the back of your mind that shapes the health and success of your love life. The goal of Step 1 is to *identify* what is in your psychological love life so you can decide what to change. There are three (3) parts to everyone's psychological love life:

- Memories of the *relationship experiences* you've had in love starting from the very beginning of your life;
- What you've *learned about love relationships* from those relationship experiences;
- *Aftereffects of those relationship experiences*, especially if they were hurtful and unhealthy.

To help you figure out each one of these three parts of your particular psychological love life, I've listed once again the ten (10) most common unhealthy relationship experiences that negatively affect an adult person's love life:

	Exposed to	Affects my love life
Abandonment		
Abuse		
Control		
Dependency		
Dishonesty		
Exploitation		
Mistrust		
Neglect		
Rejection		
Self-centeredness		

1. **Identify the unhealthy relationship experiences you've been exposed to starting from the very beginning of your life.**

Slowly read through the above list of unhealthy relationship experiences. **Check off the ones you were exposed to in your life (i.e., Exposed to).** Remember, your love life started the day you were born, so you want to think in terms of your whole life up to now (i.e. family of origin relationships are the first *love* relationships). This list is a sample of the most common unhealthy relationship experiences we found in our love life research, and it's quite possible you could add others.

Also, there may be experiences in the list that you were exposed to, but have not negatively affected your love life. To determine which experiences negatively affected your love relationships, you will have to *reflect on whether or not a particular unhealthy relationship experience is being repeated and replicated in your love life.*

For example, if you were exposed to abandonment as an adult or while growing up (e.g. a love partner abruptly left you as an adult and/or a parent abandoned your family when you were a child), and your adult love relationships tend to be with abandoning men or women, one after the other, chances are abandonment has had a negative and controlling effect on your love life. On the other hand, you could have been exposed to abandonment earlier in life, and it does not show up repetitively in the love life disappointments you've experienced.

Next, check off the unhealthy relationship experiences that are active in your love relationships (i.e., Affects my love life). This will give you a starting point to begin identifying what needs to be changed in your love relationships.

2. Identify what you've learned about love relationships from the unhealthy relationship experiences affecting your love life.

Believe it or not, if you are repeating and replicating unhealthy relationship experiences in your love life, you've probably learned something unhealthy about love relationships from them and you don't even know it.

Remember, our research showed us that what people generally learn about love relationships from unhealthy relationship experiences exists in three (3) different categories: *beliefs, behavior,* and *feelings.* In other words, what you believe about love relationships, how you behave in them, and what you feel in love relationships.

For example, if you were exposed to neglect in a relationship with someone you fell in love with as an adult, or were exposed to neglect by one or both parents growing up, there's a good chance you will believe, someone is always neglected in love. In love relationships you will either find love partners who are neglectful or neglect your love partner yourself, or both, and you will probably be pretty familiar with the feeling of deprivation in love.

Your beliefs, behavior, and feelings in love will be hidden even from you at first, but not for long if you know what you're looking for. With the unhealthy relationship experiences that affected your love life in mind, reflect on what you believe about love, how you behave in love relationships, and feel about love, to make those unhealthy relationship experiences reoccur in your love life. Use the list of unhealthy relationship experiences below to help guide you:

Abandonment

Unhealthy relationship experience affecting my love life: *abandonment*

In love relationships, I believe someone always gets *abandoned*

In love relationships, *I abandon* or the *person I love abandons me*

In love relationships, someone always feels *loss*

Abuse

Unhealthy relationship experience affecting my love life: *abuse*

In love relationships, I believe someone always gets *abused*

In love relationships, *I abuse* or the *person I love abuses me*

In love relationships, someone always feels *fear*

Control

Unhealthy relationship experience affecting my love life: *control*

In love relationships, I believe someone always gets *controlled*

In love relationships, *I control* or the *person I love controls me*

In love relationships, someone always feels *trapped*

Dependency

Unhealthy relationship experience affecting my love life: *dependency*

In love relationships, I believe someone is always *needy*

In love relationships, *I depend* or the *person I love depends on me*

In love relationships, someone always feels *needy*

Dishonesty

Unhealthy relationship experience affecting my love life: *dishonesty*

In love relationships, I believe someone is always *lied to*

In love relationships, *I lie* or the *person I love lies to me*

In love relationships, someone always feels *deceived*

Exploitation

Unhealthy relationship experience affecting my love life: *exploitation*

In love relationships, I believe someone always gets *used*

In love relationships, *I exploit* or the *person I love exploits me*

In love relationships, someone always feels *used*

Mistrust

Unhealthy relationship experience affecting my love life: *mistrust*

In love relationships, I believe someone is always *suspicious*

In love relationships, *I mistrust* or the *person I love mistrusts me*

In love relationships, someone always feels *suspicious*

Neglect

Unhealthy relationship experience affecting my love life: *neglect*

In love relationships, I believe someone always gets *neglected*

In love relationships, *I neglect* or the *person I love neglects me*

In love relationships, someone always feels *deprived*

Rejection

Unhealthy relationship experience affecting my love life: *rejection*

In love relationships, someone always gets *rejected*

In love relationships, *I reject* or the *person I love rejects me*

In love relationships, someone always feels *rejected*

Self-centeredness

Unhealthy relationship experience affecting my love life: ***self-centered***

In love relationships, I believe someone is always ***self-centered***

In love relationships, ***I'm self-centered*** or ***the person I love is self-centered***

In love, someone always feels ***insignificant***

Use the following fill-in-the-blanks to determine which of the unhealthy relationship experiences above have affected your love life, and what you've learned from them. **Go ahead, list the unhealthy relationship experiences that have affected your love life and what you've learned from them in the spaces below:**

Unhealthy relationship experience affecting my love life: _____

In love, someone always gets _____

In love, I _____ or the person I love _____ me

In love, someone always feels _____

Unhealthy relationship experience affecting my love life: _____

In love, someone always gets _____

In love, I _____ or the person I love _____ me

In love, someone always feels _____

Unhealthy relationship experience affecting my love life: _____

In love, someone always gets _____

In love, I _____ or the person I love _____ me

In love, someone always feels _____

Unhealthy relationship experience affecting my love life: _____

In love, someone always gets _____

In love, I _____ or the person I love _____ me

In love, someone always feels _____

3. Identify the aftereffects of your unhealthy relationship experience

Because unhealthy relationship experiences are usually hurtful, aftereffects occur to protect us from more hurt. Aftereffects however interfere with making healthy improvements in a love life. Step 1 includes identifying your love life aftereffects. As I mentioned earlier, there are two primary aftereffects of unhealthy relationship experience. The first is:

A. Changing your partner, instead of yourself

Think about whether or not you're trying to change your partner to make him or her more compatible, or you're changing partners one after another in temporary love relationships in an effort to find the "right one."

If you are trying to change a particular partner, the range for how this might be accomplished goes from *force*, to *manipulation*, to *fixing* or *rescuing* the person, to a simple but persistent *expectation* that your partner *should* change. If you are changing partners, one after the other, chances are your love relationships are time limited, with people coming and going, as you search for the "better" partner.

B. Defensiveness, avoiding vulnerability

As described, the second type of aftereffect that is very common as a way of coping with hurt in love relationships involves being *defensive* in love relationships. When you're defensive you're on guard against hurt. There are a million and one ways to defend yourself against getting hurt in love.

The bottom line is, *when you are defensive in a love relationship, you're protecting yourself from hurt and avoiding vulnerability.*

There are three (3) general categories of defense in a love life. You can be *distant in your love relationships, always ready to fight in your love relationships*, or *avoiding love relationships altogether.*

To complete Step 1 of the Unlearning Method, think about which aftereffects are occurring in your love life. **Now, check the aftereffects that apply to your love life:**

I try to change the person I love in my love relationships _____

I go from one person to another to try to improve my love life _____

I'm defensive in love by keeping my distance in a relationship _____

I'm defensive in love by frequently fighting with the person I love _____

I'm defensive in love by avoiding love relationships altogether _____

At this point, you should now be able to identify what is in your psychological love life. The unhealthy relationship experiences you were exposed to that are negatively affecting your love life, what you've learned from them, and aftereffects.

Good job! You've identified your psychological love life, the "blueprint" in your mind that recreates what happens in your love relationships. You now know what you need to work on to improve your love life. Let's move on to Step 2 and start *unlearning what you've learned that was unhealthy.*

Step 2 - Challenging Your Psychological Love Life

Now that you have successfully identified what is in your psychological love life, Step 2 is about *challenging* its uncontrolled dominance in your love life. Remember, your love life belongs to you, not some past relationship experience, or someone else's love life, it belongs to you, and only you. Challenging how your love life is shaped by your relationship experiences in life separates and differentiates your love life from everyone else's and begins to put you in control of your love life.

The objective is to *disrupt* the unhealthy ways your love life is being influenced by what you've experienced in love relationships from the beginning of your life. Because these influences are "learned" it is now possible to "unlearn" them and "learn or re-learn" something better. In Step 2 we'll focus on the unlearning part. Now that you've identified what is in your psychological love life, challenging how your love life is functioning starts the unlearning process.

1. Challenging your unhealthy relationship experiences

Using what you now know about the unhealthy relationship experiences that have negatively affected your love life, your objective in Step 2 is to *disrupt any and all unhealthy repetitive experience in your love life*. If something unhealthy is happening over and over again, like finding the same kind of hurtful love partner or making the same kind of love life mistake, it's time to stop and reflect on what is in control of your love life.

Once you see the *repetition*, think about what that repetition could be *replicating* in your current relationship experience. For example, if I grew up with a needy parent I had to take care of, and now in adulthood I find needy love partners to take care of, chances are I am *replicating* my earlier relationship experience with my parent in my current adult love life.

In most instances, *repetitive love life experience is replicating some kind of past relationship experience. Seeing the connections between your past relationship experience and what is happening in your present love life empowers you to make the needed changes in your love life. Remember, all of this is learned, so it can be unlearned and something healthier learned or relearned, putting you in control of your love life.*

2. Challenging what you've learned about love relationships

You are repeating and replicating unhealthy relationship experiences because you've learned something about love relationships that compels you to repeat and replicate those experiences. The more you know what you've learned, the better able you'll be to make changes, take control, and improve your love life.

Remember, clarifying your *beliefs*, *behavior* and *feelings* in love will tell you what you've learned about love relationships. For example, if you were exposed to dishonesty in your love life, chances are you'll unconsciously believe that dishonesty is inevitable in a love relationship. You'll also either find someone who lies or lie yourself in love, and be familiar with and expect the feeling of deception in love relationships. Remember, all of this learning is out of your awareness at first, until you've identified its repetition and replication in your adult love life.

In Step 2 you take what you now know about what you've learned, the beliefs, behavior, and feelings associated with whichever unhealthy relationship experience is affecting your love life, and challenge its ability to dominate your love relationships. This new therapeutic attitude will make the "space" (separate from the past) necessary in your love life for something "new" (different) to take its place. We human beings have to unlearn something we've learned before we can learn or relearn something new.

Let's look again at the dishonesty example I just gave you. Challenging dishonesty in your love life because you were exposed to dishonesty growing up or in an adult love relationship would involve your understanding that dishonesty is unhealthy and is ruining your chances of finding and sustaining a healthy love relationship. Your challenge would be to disrupt how dishonesty has settled into your love life, keeping an eye on your beliefs, behavior, and feelings in love life situations.

Remember, one of the great things about being a human being and having a "mind" is that the healthy part of your mind can realize that another part is unhealthy and decide to do something about it. If we strengthen the healthy part over time, it can eventually keep the unhealthy part from dominating what we believe, do, and feel in our lives.

Same here, what you were exposed to in love in your life if it was unhealthy could be dominating your love life. Our objective in Step 2 is to strengthen your ability to challenge and disrupt that dominance so you can have a healthier and more successful love life.

3. Challenging aftereffects of your unhealthy relationship experience

Recall that the reason why aftereffects even exist in your love life is because the unhealthy relationship experiences that got into your love life can "hurt." Aftereffects are the ways people protect themselves from being hurt again.

The problem is these aftereffects can interfere with making the improvements we're talking about. They need to be "undone."

Remember, the two primary aftereffects are *trying to change your love partner* and *defensiveness in love.*

A. Challenging your efforts to change your love partner

If you are going through potential partners, one after another, you are probably searching for something that doesn't exist. The underlying motivation is to keep love relationships superficial because they were hurtful when they were allowed to get deeper in the past. If that underlying fear of getting hurt again is not "cured," you can see how a love life could suffer from not being allowed to deepen over the course of your life.

On the other hand, if you are trying to change the person you've fallen in love with, there is no chance of success. You simply cannot change another person. You'll only get resistance and resentment for not accepting your partner for who he or she is. Accepting him or her, or leaving the relationship, are your only two options. Unfortunately, trying to change people in love is a very common practice that creates a lot of misery for a lot of people.

It's time to realize, it's impossible to change another person, and going through multiple partners is a sign that something is not working in your psychological love life. Look for the evidence that you've been trying to force changes in the people you've fallen in love with, or manipulate changes, fix or rescue them, or you simply used your expectations to influence the people you've been in love with. If you can convince yourself it's time to stop this unhealthy way of coping with the pains of love, you'll challenge yourself, and make a space for something new to happen.

B. Challenging your defensiveness in love

Step 2 ends when you get good at challenging your defensiveness in love. Take a closer look at how open you let yourself be when in love. Are you self-protective in a love relationship? Are you always expecting to get hurt and needing to defend yourself whenever you feel vulnerable? If you realize that defensiveness in love always interferes with giving and receiving love in a love relationship, you might think twice about defensiveness. Ask yourself, what's the worst thing that could happen?

Let's say you've made a decision, based on a lot of forethought and consideration, that you're going to jump into a love relationship with someone you've fallen in love with. Unfortunately, you can't know ahead of time whether or not it will work out and mature into a lifelong relationship. Best you can do is check the person out, acknowledging to yourself that you are in love and that the person you're in love with is emotionally available. The rest is an inevitable risk. No risk, no gain.

If it doesn't work out, yes, you'll be disappointed and probably hurt, but you can heal and learn something about love relationships so the next time you fall in love you'll be wiser and the experience could be more successful. If you have faith in your innate ability to *heal loss,* you'll be better able to tolerate the unpredictability of love. Unfortunately, there is no way to get around the hurt. *Remember, you simply can't play in the field of love without risking the possibility of loss.* Of course, there are also little hurts that come from the mere fact that there are always two unique individuals in a love relationship, two different perspectives, and the inevitable possibility of disagreement. In the long run, working out differences and disagreements may hurt a little but the learning that takes place and the evolution of intimacy in the relationship makes it all worthwhile.

Challenge your defensiveness in love whenever you see it emerge in a love relationship, and try to take feedback seriously if people are pointing out to you that you're defensive in love. Very often, our love partners and other people will see unnecessary defensiveness long before we do. Our focus here is on doing what we can individually in our own minds to diminish defensiveness so an emotional space can be opened up for something new and better to happen in our love lives.

Step 3 - Practice the Healthy Opposite of Your Psychological Love Life

The third and final Step 3 brings us to what I like to call the "antidote" for the "toxic" unhealthy relationship experiences that have negatively affected your love life. Once you've identified what is in your psychological love life (i.e. unhealthy relationship experiences you were exposed to, what you've learned from them, and aftereffects), and you have successfully begun challenging the control they have had over your love life, it's time to *learn (or relearn) and practice something healthier.*

An easy and simple way to determine what is healthier is to adopt the *opposite* of the unhealthy relationship experiences you were exposed to. To help you do this I've listed the ten (10) unhealthy relationship experiences again along with their defined "opposites." **Check the healthy relationship experiences that apply to your love life:**

> Abandonment → **ATTACHMENT** _____
>
> Abuse → **RESPECT** _____
>
> Control → **FREEDOM** _____
>
> Dependency → **INDEPENDENCE** _____
>
> Dishonesty → **HONESTY** _____
>
> Exploitation → **CONSIDERATION** _____
>
> Mistrust → **TRUST** _____
>
> Neglect → **DEVOTION** _____
>
> Rejection → **ACCEPTANCE** _____
>
> Self-centeredness → **INTIMACY** _____

Consider these opposite experiences as potential *corrections* for the unhealthy relationship experiences you were exposed to. In fact, if you go down the list and check off the ones that got into your love life, you'll also have a list of their opposites. For example, if you were exposed to rejection growing up in your family or in adult love relationships, the opposite corrective experience for rejection is "acceptance." Practicing acceptance in your love relationships establishes an ongoing "correction" for the negative effect rejection has had on your love life.

The objective of Step 3 is first to gather the opposites of the unhealthy relationship experiences you were exposed to. These opposite "positive" love relationship experiences are tailored to your particular constellation of unhealthy relationship experiences. Say you were exposed to rejection, dependency, and neglect, and all three found their way into your love life. Then your constellation of unhealthy relationship experiences would be: rejection, dependency, and neglect. The opposites tailored for your particular love life would be: acceptance, independence, and devotion.

Here's the point, using the above example, if you were to decide to *practice in every way possible*, acceptance, independence, and devotion in your love life, you would be "correcting" the ill effects of earlier unhealthy relationship experiences on your particular adult love relationships. You now have accurate personalized information about your psychological love life, that you can use to effectively work on improving your adult love life going forward.

Let's make this clearer and define what I mean when I say, *practice in every way possible*. If you know what the *antidote* (i.e. healthier relationship experience) is to the *toxic* (i.e. unhealthy relationship experience) you've been exposed to that has negatively affected your love life choices and success, you can practice finding these healthy relationship experiences in your love life. *You do it by looking for them in the partners you select, and practicing them in what you believe, do, and feel in your love life.*

Continuing with the above example, once you are convinced that the "unfamiliar" (i.e. literally referring to what was not taught to you in your "family") experiences of acceptance, independence, and devotion will permanently improve your love life, you're going to make sure that your present and future love relationships have plenty of these three experiences in them. Also, what you learn from these healthier experiences could be *new learning* or something you have had to *relearn*. Again, a good example of relearning is the ability to trust. Trust is indeed something you came into the world with. Unfortunately, your relationship experiences could have persuaded you to give up trusting. If this were the case, you'd have to relearn how to trust to get it back. Now let's apply Step 3 to the three (3) parts of your psychological love life: your relationship experiences, what you've learned from your relationship experiences, and any aftereffects of what you've experienced and learned.

1. Practice healthier opposite relationship experiences

Remember, I gave you a list of ten (10) *unhealthy relationship experiences* and ten (10) *opposite healthy relationship experiences.* You've picked the corresponding opposite experiences that go with the unhealthy relationship experiences that have gotten into your love life. Practicing those healthy relationship experiences that match your unhealthy relationship experiences will eventually begin to "correct" the negative effects of repeating and replicating unhealthy relationship experiences.

Don't forget, you'll practice your healthy relationship experiences by making sure your love partners are also practicing them, and you'll make sure your love relationships always have a good measure of each. For example, if I grew up negatively influenced by dishonesty and found love partners one after another who cheated on me, my correction would be to practice honesty in my love life. I would need to make sure that I consciously look for real evidence of honesty in my choice of love partner along with developing a commitment to honesty in relationship with him or her.

2. Practice learning healthier lessons about love relationships

It is inevitable that you will learn healthier lessons about love relationships from the healthier opposite relationship experiences you'll have. Healthier *beliefs* about love relationships, along with what *you do in love* and/or what another person *does to you in love,* will create healthier *feelings* in your love relationships. You are now in control of your love life because you are able to determine what is healthy or not, effective or not, in your love relationships. And this is really the whole point of our Unlearning Method, to return control of your love life back to you.

3. Practice undoing your aftereffects

Finally, you're at the end of the unlearning method. Your final objective is to undo the aftereffects that have been blocking the needed changes in your love life. As we did earlier, let's look at each aftereffect individually.

A. Practice the opposite of trying to change the person you love

Let's say in the course of applying this Unlearning Method you've identified this particular aftereffect in your own personal psychological love life, challenged it, and you are now in the position to undo it. How? *By changing yourself if you want to change your love life.* Wait a minute. How does that work? We now know you've been trying to change love partners to deal with your chronic love life difficulties and realized that's not going to work. Remember, the only person you can change is yourself, that is, if you are properly motivated to do so. I'll assume by this time that you are pretty motivated to change your love life. Going just a little further, realize if you sincerely want to change your love life, your only recourse is to change yourself.

Chances are you've made this simple observation. If you've been working on applying this Unlearning Method to your love life, and you've gotten this far, then you've already realized that our Unlearning Method changes love lives from the *inside out.* It's the goings on in your psychological love life that matter the most. Unfortunately, there are plenty of people who learn this lesson the hard way after years of trying to change the people they fall in love with, or some superficial aspect of their love lives (e.g. what they wear, where they go, how they say, what they say, etc.).

B. Practice the opposite of your defensiveness in love

I hate to start off with a dirty word, but the opposite of defensiveness is *vulnerability*. Seriously, it's time to practice being vulnerable in your love relationship. If you don't like the word vulnerable, we can use *open*, practice being open in your love relationship. When you are being vulnerable or open in love, you are allowing another person to get in, to really know you. The advantage is, this is a relationship where you can simply be yourself. The relief in that is, without a doubt, so healthy and therapeutic.

The point is, you now realize that your defensiveness keeps you closed (opposite of open) and unable to give and receive love. OK, maybe you'll give and get some love even if you are defensive, but much less than you deserve. And remember our earlier discussion, *defensiveness in love is really telling the world you've been hurt in love and it's not yet resolved.*

Putting all the pieces together, while you are being open or vulnerable, you'll need to remember, in love getting hurt unintentionally is a distinct possibility. However, you'll have to remind yourself that you can and will be able to tolerate the potential hurts of love (for a good cause) and heal them. Knowing this fact about you makes taking a risk on love a lot easier.

CHAPTER 5

My Psychological Love Life

Who Taught Me About Love Relationships?

I figure the best way to give my readers a clear and understandable example of how our Unlearning Method can transform a love life is to use my own love life as an illustration. You should know that the original reason for getting into this love life research was my personal experience of having my love life change during the course of my personal therapy. I kept a series of journals during the eight years I was in weekly psychoanalysis with Dr. Benjamin Wolstein. I would write down the various insights and understandings as they were revealed to me throughout the course of my treatment.

My journals helped me form an overview of what was happening to me as I changed and developed myself. As a consequence, I noticed a pattern of change in the area of my love life that was particularly important to me. I had been stuck making the same mistakes over and over again and feeling very disappointed in my love life. The changes my love life went through as a result of my therapy experience became the source of information I needed to extract the understanding I could then offer my own patients more efficiently and in a shorter period of time.

As you read through the description of my love life experience, how I changed my psychological love life, and improved the overall health of my love relationships, you'll see the points of similarity with the Unlearning Method discussed in this book. I believe that knowledge derived from one's own experience in life is the most meaningful. I know this system of changing your psychological love life, as a method of making permanent improvements in your ability to find and sustain a healthy love relationship, works; my own love life is living proof. Once I was able to identify my psychological love life, challenge what I had learned that was unhealthy, and practice finding and sustaining healthier experiences and learning, my love life improved.

Dr. Benjamin Wolstein, my psychoanalyst, guided me through these changes and I have come to realize and appreciate his wisdom and understanding of the healthy and unhealthy love relationship. Although he never wrote an article or book about the psychology of the love relationship in his lifetime, I am forever grateful for the knowledge and personal experiences about the interpersonal relationship in love that he shared in the course of my treatment with him.

I'm sure you've heard the old adage a picture is worth a thousand words. Well here's a photo of Dad, Mom and me at a little over a year old. My answer to the question, who taught me about love relationships is, Dad and Mom, or more specifically as I have come to realize, for me Mom more than Dad.

My parents, Manual and Hilda Jordan, were the first-generation children of immigrant parents who came to this country from Sao Miguel, Azores in the early 20th century. They settled in New Bedford, Massachusetts, at the time a Portuguese enclave. My mother was the only surviving child out of six. All the other babies were male and died as stillbirths, miscarriages, crib deaths, with one son dying of a childhood illness at a year and a half. My mother's father was determined to have a son or two to carry his name and work in his ethnic grocery store. As a consequence of multiple losses and unresolved grief, my mother's parents held onto their daughter keeping her close to home by any means possible (i.e. control and guilt) even after her marriage and birthing four children of her own. In effect, my mother never physically or emotionally separated from her parents during the course of their lifetimes. She lived on the first floor in her father's house with her husband who worked for her father and their four sons. My parents were married for over 70 years.

My Parents & Me

Step 1: Identifying My Unhealthy Psychological Love Life

Identifying My Unhealthy Relationship Experiences

My relationship experiences growing up were mostly healthy from my father and mostly unhealthy from my mother. My father was a devoted, hard-working man, who attached to his family, but struggled with personal immaturities and self-neglect. He often complained about the absence of separation from his wife's parents, reminding himself that due to an 8th grade education working for his father-in-law was a better option than trying to make it on his own. Once married, I realized that my father's influence on my love life came in the form of an ability to form and keep a commitment, a devotion to work and providing for a family, and an unhealthy self-neglect which promoted a self-sacrificing care-taking orientation in my love relationships.

My mother's influence, however, proved to be of greater importance with respect to the health of my love life. She was dependent, controlling, and at times self-centered as a way to counter the weight of her parents' emotional demands. As time progressed, she became frequently frustrated and angry, and on occasion was physically abusive when her children were young. Over time, I became more and more interested in and felt more and more responsible for my mother's unresolved emotional pain. I spent much of my late childhood and adolescence talking privately with my mother about her chronic unhappiness. Our relationship became my way of coping with her volatility.

As I grew older and her emotional pain more clearly expressed, I tried to "fix" (with no success) her difficulties with recurrent "psychological" advice and explanations. Our occasional relationship reversal (i.e. she is the child, I am the parent) became more pronounced as my role became more "parentified" (Jurkovic 1997). We'll get back to the relevance of this reversal later on. Eventually, when it was time to leave home for college, her dependency on our relationship was a source of significant feelings of loss for her. She tried to stop me from leaving home without success.

Of all the maternal relationship influences in my early life, *dependency* and *control* were the most potent, negatively affecting my ability to find and sustain a healthy love relationship in adulthood. In my early 30's, Wolstein shared an observation with me in one of our sessions, that I was using my relationship with my mother as a "template" in my efforts to find a love relationship.

This realization, brought to my awareness by my therapist, was shocking to say the least. I had absolutely no consciousness of the fact that I was doing so. I began to realize that I was looking for *dependent women* as the *familiar prototype* for a love relationship. To add insult to injury, I further realized that in many instances I would assume that dependency existed in a person I would meet, even when it did not. In some instances, I found, gravitated toward, or was attracted to an emotionally dependent woman as if I had some kind of detection ability (e.g. radar). In other instances, I met people who were clearly not (not with me at least) dependent and controlling but I assumed they were and acted, at least in my own thoughts and feelings, as though they were.

During this period in my single life (i.e. late 20's to early 30's), which I refer to as my "serial monogamy" days, I met one woman after another for committed love relationships that generally lasted from one to three years, never longer. When dependency needs emerged in the women who were dependent, or any emotional need like a natural desire to attach in those who weren't dependent, I reacted with *fears of being controlled* and began to withdraw in and from the relationship. In my mind and heart, dependency (real or virtual) was associated with stifling control and I had to leave. I went through this cycle a number of times throughout this period with short hiatuses in between, generating more and more disappointment, feelings of loss, unresolved hurt, and defensive distancing as time progressed.

Identify What I Learned from My Unhealthy Relationship Experience

First and foremost, I learned to *believe* and expect that all eligible women were dependent and controlling. Looking back, I was so convinced of this, simply because it was what I was familiar with. I have always been fascinated with the root meaning of words. In the case of "familiar" the root is "family." What we learn in our families shapes our experience of interpersonal reality when we become adults. In my case, the two women in my life growing up were dependent and controlling (i.e. my mother and her mother). With the help of "stereotypic" thinking, generalizing from two to all women, I expected to find dependency and control even, as I noted earlier, if it wasn't there. In so many instances I have heard people say things like, "All men are cheaters," or "All women are bitchy." Where hurtful unresolved relationship experiences were the source from which a patient discouraged him or herself from dating again after a previous relationship was painfully lost. For me at that time, all eligible women, regardless of any other qualities they might have had, were believed to be just like my mother, dependent and controlling, end of story.

When out and about, mingling with people, looking for a love relationship, I was acting on my unconscious belief that all eligible women were dependent and controlling. In my case, I *behaved* in such a way as to increase the probability of finding a dependent woman. I would often encourage people I met to tell me stories about their life and experiences. People in need of understanding or help were on occasion attracted to my interest and this scenario became the primary way I met women during this period of my single life. In effect, I was recreating the interpersonal relationship I had with my dependent mother whenever possible with any woman I met, without the least bit of awareness that I was doing so.

The *feelings* these experiences recreated for me completed the meeting and dating scenario I was familiar with. I looked for any and all evidence of "neediness" in the women I talked to. As I said earlier, I often mistook other feelings for neediness and on more than one occasion expected neediness in a woman that did not experience this feeling. I now understand that neediness is the feeling that dependency generates and I unconsciously expected it to show up when meeting women. Under the spell of what I had learned about love relationships as a consequence of my mother's dependency, neediness was recreated and mixed with whatever emotion of love there was.

Beyond neediness, the first feeling I expected to have was the feeling of being "trapped." In my psychological love life, dependency recreates the feeling of neediness, and control recreates the feeling of being trapped in it. Earlier in my life I had experienced my mother's neediness as a trap

I struggled to survive in. Too young to leave, I believed I had to come up with innovative and creative ways of tolerating her feeling of neediness and the trapped feeling it created. As an adult, I learned to disengage when I felt trapped, something I could not do until it came time to leave home for college -- a situation, as I indicated earlier, my mother didn't like very much given her dependency on me. At twenty years of age, my father was instrumental in helping me emotionally separate from my mother and move away to college, leaving home for good. I was never quite sure what the emotional consequences were for him for the help he gave me.

Identifying Aftereffects of My Unhealthy Relationship Experiences

Of course, then there are the aftereffects. For me, the most innovative, creative coping response I could come up with was to develop my ability to listen and advise my dependent mother. Somehow, rising to the role of my mother's confident made me feel less trapped. In my adolescence, I began reading psychology, psychiatry, and self-help books to educate myself to increase the chances of saying something of value to my dependent and frequently depressed, frustrated, and on occasion, angry mother. I became convinced that I could *fix her* if I could find the right book to dispense the right advice.

My mother and I met frequently, at some points daily, to discuss her feelings which ranged from disappointments about her parents, her dream of separating from them, her disappointment that my father didn't force the issue, her ambivalence about leaving her parents, her anger about being "forced" to work down "the store" (family business), and more. Most of these "sessions" consisted of my mother venting her unhappiness, listening to my advice without ever making changes, and airing her secret desire to openly oppose my grandfather and my father. If anyone showed up during one of these "sessions" she and I would immediately stop talking, and neither one of us ever shared the content of what was talked about with anyone else.

Later in my life, as my professional training progressed, these "sessions" with my mother stopped. As I mentioned earlier, I became aware of my "parentification" (Jurkovic, 1997), a term that describes the transformation of a child into a parent with a parent. My mother's dependency had set in motion a change in our relationship, where I assumed the position of parent when I listened to my mother's emotional pains and offered her solutions to alleviate (fix) her suffering. I came to understand that my parentification was an immature effort to cope with the fact that I needed love from my dependent mother. Attempting to fix my mother felt like a better option for me than depression or anger, and permitted me to hang onto the personal fantasy that at some point I would succeed in fixing her and get the love that was owed to me. That never happened.

Parentification in my childhood, found its way into my adult love life in the form of harboring fantasies of "fixing" any woman I was in a love relationship with. Even if I had little to offer during my graduate school years, for example, I still hung onto the thought that I could listen and dispense the right advice and fix my love partner's emotional problems. Familiarity is tenacious. Again, some of the women I met during this period in my life were suffering in their own ways, others were not, yet I assumed they were all dependent and in need of "fixing." Clearly a recapitulation of my relationship with my mother. Amazing how I remained unconscious of that fact until Dr. Wolstein pointed it out.

The final aspect of my psychological love life that I identified was the ways in which I was defending myself in my love relationships by *distancing*. Remember, distancing is defined as being in a love relationship at a distance. Filling out the details of my love life at the time, I discovered that I was also coping with the accumulation of unresolved hurt and loss by getting into love relationships but keeping my distance. I did that in a myriad of ways, from keeping my feelings to myself, to limiting the number of times I would see someone in a week, to finding ways to disengage while with someone (i.e. emotional detachment) and more. Distancing was a perfect way of blunting the anticipated effects of too much intimacy. In fact, distancing in a love relationship also predicts departure under the right conditions. For me, the right conditions were a growing feeling of being trapped by someone's emerging neediness. Nevertheless, the problem with distancing in a love relationship is it tends to generate dissatisfaction both for the person practicing it and the person on the receiving end.

Step 2: Challenging My Unhealthy Psychological Love Life

Challenging My Unhealthy Repetitions and Replications

Once I became aware of the unhealthy relationship experiences that got into my adult love life, what I learned from them, and the aftereffects that formed to help me cope with what I had learned, I started noticing that I was repeating and replicating what I had learned in all my interactions with women. This newly formed consciousness, prompted by the reflections shared by my therapist, helped me realize that I had to *challenge* and *disrupt* the hold my unhealthy learning had over my love life. My love life simply felt out of my control. I didn't know this at the time but the way I challenged what I had learned was to stop dating for a while, until I could figure out how to fix my own love life. During this period, I remember looking at women like they were from another planet. I had lost trust in my own ability to meet and relate to members of the opposite sex in a healthy way.

Challenging My Unhealthy Beliefs, Behavior, and Feelings

I began to re-evaluate what I believed about women. Realizing that it made no sense to expect that all women were dependent and controlling. In social situations where I would meet new people, I began noticing the type of women I was attracted to. Like a habit reinforced by my beliefs and behavior, I began to strengthen my ability to stop myself from doing what was "familiar" and unhealthy. I also began to understand that neediness and feeling trapped were not the healthiest feelings to have in a love relationship. I challenged myself with an awareness that it was time to separate from what I had learned in my family of origin and differentiate what I needed and wanted in my own love life from what my mother had unwittingly taught me about love relationships.

Challenging My Unhealthy Aftereffects

I also began to challenge the ways I had developed to *cope with* and *accommodate to* the neediness and trapped feelings I experienced in my love relationships. These were aftereffects of what I had learned from my unhealthy relationship experiences. I became realistic about wanting to change any person I fell in love with. It's never going to happen. No one has the power to change another person in or out of love. I realized that the only thing I get in this effort to change the person I love is *resistance* and *resentment*. Resistance because the person I try to change reacts by resisting my efforts as an experienced affront, whether expressed or silently felt.

Of course, people can "act like" someone else is responsible for a change he or she has made, but that's acting. As an individual, it is only possible to change yourself. Resentment, on the other hand, occurs because when I was trying to change the person I loved, I was not accepting her as she is. Again, as individuals we all possess a sensitivity to not being accepted as "good enough," expressed or silently felt. I realized I was damaging my love relationships and promoting resistance and resentment by believing in and trying to change people.

The other aftereffect I began challenging in my love life was the *distance* I kept in a love relationship. I wasn't allowing people to get close enough to me, even though it might have looked like I was. Years of accumulated hurt and loss had taken its toll. Distance was the defense mechanism I was using to protect myself from additional hurt and vulnerability. I realized in multiple moments of honest personal reflection that distancing in my love relationships was interfering with my ability to give and receive love. I was now alone but aware that some things needed to change in my love life if I was going to be able to find and sustain a healthy love relationship. I knew I had to take control of my love life and the way to do this was to work on my psychological love life.

Step 3: Practicing Healthy Opposite Relationship Experiences

Practicing My Healthy Opposite Experiences

The last step in the transformation of my psychological love life came as a consequence of realizing something different had to happen in my love life. Again, without an awareness of the true purpose of the changes I was making at the time, I made a few novel friendships with several women I met. One in particular became a "best friend." No sex, no romance, just true friendship. Looking back, these friendships were like the "emotional internship" I needed to learn some new things about women. Some things my mother had never taught me. More specifically, that a woman could be *independent* and *not controlling* in a relationship. My new best friend was independent and not controlling. I learned in that relationship that a woman could live and love without neediness. I also learned that when a woman feels secure about herself as a person, control in a relationship was never necessary.

Practicing New Learning in My Love Life

These important new lessons were the *opposite* of what I had learned growing up. I now had to *practice* them in my relationships with women. Practice being the way to fortify new healthy learning and erode the influence of old unhealthy learning. I believed in a stereotypic fashion that all women were dependent and controlling. I now needed to understand and repeatedly apply my new understanding that "many women" are independent and free (not controlling).

I needed to expand my view of love relationships to include the idea that there is a mixture of people out there in the world. Not all people are alike, regardless of what my earlier experiences in life taught me. I began to understand and apply the notion that we are all individuals and essentially unique. This idea helped me challenge the stereotypic thinking that had reinforced my unhealthy unconscious view of women as dependent and controlling, and practice a more varied and accurate perspective.

During this period, I also seemed to be developing a "relationship mind set." Thinking of some women as independent and free, I practiced being able to determine who was needy and controlling, and who was independent and free whenever I met new people. I paid closer attention to the personalities of the people I met, wondering who was "available for a love relationship" and who was not. Prior to this, being in a relationship with a unique individual who was deemed to be emotionally available was not really the objective. Loving an independent woman who did not have to control the relationship was a lot easier and healthier. I realized this fact, first in my friendships and later in a love relationship that would grow from my own development and emotional availability.

Undoing My Love Life Aftereffects

I was now able to practice *changing myself in order to change my love life*. I was convinced that trying to change another person was futile. Upon closer examination of my relationship experiences, there were too many instances of resistance and resentment to ignore. I even became aware of the way in which changing myself might influence the person I was in love with. My wife Victoria is currently an avid road bike rider. However, there was a time when she rode a heavy commuting bike once in a while without any real interest in road biking.

I became increasingly interested in road bikes and purchased an expensive carbon bike with accessories and road biking apparel for myself. I tried repeatedly to convince her to join me, offering to buy her a better bike with accessories and a biking uniform. She resisted repeatedly, until I had to remind myself that I was back to my old habit of trying to change the person I'm in love with. I gave it up and rode on my own accepting that my wife was satisfied with the bike she had.

Every once in a while, Victoria would ask me about my plans to go biking. Her curiosity increased in my biking activities as my interest in changing her diminished. At a certain point she approached me requesting a new bike with all the extras. Surprised I asked her if she wanted a newer version of the bike she already had. She insisted that we buy a bike like mine with road biking apparel and accessories. Victoria now rides on a regular basis with and without accompanying family or friends. I realized that *making healthy changes in myself in plain sight* had the effect of peeking Victoria's curiosity about biking and inviting a more active interest in biking. A wonderful yet unpredictable byproduct of changing oneself in a love relationship.

The last and final "opposite" I practiced to permanently change my love life was going from defensiveness in love, what I called "distancing," to allowing myself to be more vulnerable in my love life. Again, realizing that my defensiveness in love always inhibited my ability to love and be loved. And defensiveness is always the result of unresolved hurt that remains unresolved as long as one stays defensive. With these healthy realizations in mind, the practice of vulnerability or openness in love involved for me the following practices. The decision to *communicate hurt* whenever possible instead of converting hurt to anger or rage, which are often destructive, disguise hurt and stop hurt from healing. Along with this practice to communicate hurt, and notice I said practice because it's never easy to do, I also practiced reducing my defensive words and actions. Reminding myself I was defensive to avoid feeling vulnerable while anticipating more hurt.

Another vulnerability for me was trying to get better at *making apologies* when I was at fault instead of the defensive use of blame that always interferes with healing in a love relationship. I now know when I'm defensive apologies are impossible. Earlier, in this book I talked about having "faith" in our inherent ability to heal hurt in a love relationship. This became a practice for me as well.

I started the introduction of this book with the question, "What are the two most intense human emotions?" We agreed that love is one, and I suggested grief is the other. Being able to *grieve a loss* inevitably improves our ability to love by healing hurt in love. Becoming confident in our ability to handle the loss of love makes the risk of falling in love with its inevitable vulnerability an easier risk to take and sustain. I now practice acknowledging the importance of grief as a natural emotion and indicator of our ability to love and be loved, in my life and the lives of my patients.

Correcting My Love Life

My mother said to me a year or so before she died, "You know, you are who you are because of me." In a certain sense she was quite right. Her unintentional teaching about love relationships resulted in my years long quest to change myself and my love life. I now understand that my parents were limited by the circumstances of their lives without ever having the opportunity to become aware of and do something about the unhealthy relationship experiences they endured and how those experiences were repeated and replicated in their lives and the lives of their children. This understanding has deepened the love and appreciation I have for them and made me realize the importance of taking personal responsibility for myself and for what I've learned about love relationships in my life.

The person I married is independent and not controlling, because I realized the importance of independence and freedom in my particular love life. Victoria and I have been married for twenty-five years and counting. Change is easier when you are able to determine which opposite "corrective experiences" are necessary in your particular love life. Opposite healthy relationship experiences provide an opportunity for corrective learning and the undoing of the unhealthy aftereffects of earlier toxic experiences. My original intention in writing this book was to introduce a system of improving your love life that could be tailored to your personal experiences in love. A system of improving your love life that would be focused on your particular love life and efficiently applied without having to undergo years of psychological treatment.

I hope the ideas in this book are as useful to your love life as they have been to mine.

CHAPTER 6

Treatments For Your Love Life

Educating Your Love Life

Love Life Seminar, Love Life Webinar & LoveLifeLearningCenter.com

Remember learning is our greatest asset and greatest liability. Greatest asset because we are able to create an amazing world as a result of the transmission of knowledge from one generation to another. Greatest liability because our greatest miseries are just as often transmitted from generation to generation as the positive consequence of what we've learned. In the area of our mental and emotional health, learning plays a greater role than we currently realize. Our ability to learn is so finely tuned from the very beginnings of life that we have yet to fully appreciate the extent to which what we learn from the significant people in our lives will determine how mentally and physically healthy we will be.

This book is about learning and its intimate relationship with the health of our emotional lives, specifically our love lives. Learning is such a user-friendly function. We all know how to learn innately from the very onset of life. We can learn to improve our ability to learn, but the basic process of internalizing knowledge through experience is hard-wired. The idea of having to become aware of what was learned, to unlearn what was unhealthy, and replace what was learned with new learning and/or relearning, appeals to people as something they can do and succeed at.

As we became more involved in our love life research, we became aware of the need many people have for love life information and knowledge. As Leo Buscaglia discovered in relation to love, our society offers little in the way of education for the two most significant emotions humans are subjected to in the course of their lives: love and grief. Victoria and I developed the **Love Life Seminar** in an effort to offer interested persons an opportunity to obtain a concentrated, intensive learning experience in love life psychology. Much of the outline of this book follows the presentation of our research findings on the unhealthy love life, the discovery and exploration of the psychological love life, and our unlearning method as presented in the Love Life Seminar.

The seminar is an ideal group learning context within which to learn how to determine what was learned about love relationships, to learn how to challenge what was unhealthy, and how to practice a healthier opposite alternative. And of course, our **Love Life Webinar** is the internet version of our seminar that relies on online communication to expand our audience. Our work introduced a conscious form of remedial learning in an area of personal experience, the love life, that is traditionally left to unconscious learning in unpredictable family relationships that too often teach lessons about love that perpetuate misery and toxic relationships.

Just like Buscaglia's discovery that people, in his case his university students, needed love life teaching, my blog the **Love Life Learning Center,** launched in 2012, similarly showed me the need for love life teaching still exists. The orientation of our blog is to be an online "love life library" of accurate psychological information about love relationships. Like our Love Life Seminar, our blog emphasizes teaching people more broadly how to work on their love lives. For example, the two most popular articles on our blog are "I Love a Married Woman," and "My Husband's Narcissistic Mother." These articles address the true experience of these two very challenging love life situations that many people face and have difficulty handling. Reading the varied commentary and following the discussions on the blog has been an important part of our research and learning experience.

Short-term Learning of the Unlearning Method

Love Life Consultations

It is possible to learn how to unlearn with our Unlearning Method in a private one on one interaction with a trained professional counselor, social worker, or psychologist. We call it the **Love Life Consultation.** A Love Life Consultation is a series of 45-minute sessions that introduces a person with love life difficulties to the Unlearning Method. The primary focus of the Love Life Consultation is to teach a person Step 1 which identifies his or her psychological love life. As you will recall, our psychological love lives consist of our love relationship experiences from the beginning of our life, what we've learned from those relationship experiences, and the aftereffects of what we've experienced and learned when it was unhealthy. Persons undergoing a Love Life Consultation are guided by a consultant, a licensed mental health practitioner, in the identification of their own unique, personally defined, psychological love life.

Once a person's psychological love life has been defined, he or she is introduced to Steps 2 and 3. This part of the Unlearning Method is now possible once the psychological love life is conscious and known to the person. Step 2 involves repetitive challenges as needed of whatever is deemed unhealthy in a psychological love life. Step 3 is the practice of healthier alternative experiences and learning that corrects for what was originally learned and unhealthy.

Steps 2 and 3 are taught and examples from the person's love life explored, however, they are primarily practiced by the person on his or her own. Some people might request that their Love Life Consultation last longer in order to practice Steps 2 and 3 under the guidance of the consultant. How long beyond the required several sessions a Love Life Consultation lasts is entirely up to the person undergoing the consultation.

Removing Barriers to Learning the Unlearning Method

Love Life Focused Psychotherapy

A Love Life Consultation can transform into a Love Life Focused Psychotherapy when there are significant psychological and emotional "barriers" to learning the Unlearning Method. The existence of complications may be known ahead of time or discovered as a consequence of undergoing a Love Life Consultation. Love Life Focused Psychotherapy offers a person the reliable support and understanding necessary to work through the complications interfering with learning how to unlearn what was learned about love relationships.

Common barriers to unlearning and learning something new in the area of our psychological love lives are emotional illnesses that create depressive and/or anxiety symptoms. Treating the emotional illness first with weekly individual psychotherapy, and psychotropic medication if needed, would make it easier for a person to focus on and successfully learn how to change their love life. Personality disorders where certain behaviors are rigid, troubling, and repetitive might complicate the required learning process for many people. Improving a person's ability to be open and receptive to change will make it much easier to learn how to change his or her love life.

Sometimes abuse and trauma early in life create defensive and self-protective behavior now in adulthood that interfere with a person feeling safe enough to learn something new and healthier about love relationships. It may be necessary to work with and through the post-trauma symptoms and complications that are active now in adulthood and in large measure responsible for a disappointing love life. People interested in unlearning what they have learned about love relationships may have difficulty because they are not yet ready to "separate" and/or "differentiate" themselves from their family of origin.

Family of origin attachments and unresolved emotional immaturity can often linger well into a person's adulthood personal life and relationships. The stresses and complications they create for a person often trigger the conscious need to change his or her love life. However, these attachments and immaturity can get in the way of the changes that need to take place. This would require a period of psychotherapeutic intervention where a person is helped to separate and differentiate themselves as an individual from other members of the family, before being receptive enough to learn how to unlearn and learn something new in his or her individual love life.

Working on Your Psychological Love Lives Together

Couple/Marital Therapy

Working effectively as a couple, whether committed or married, on how the two of you relate in love would require changing your psychological love lives in each other's presence. It is a very intimate moment in a couple when two people share their psychological love lives with each other. This intimate sharing is essentially what a couple or marital therapist would be looking to create in couple therapy. In fact, much of the initial work of couple therapy is working through the defenses and aftereffects people form to cope with hurt and vulnerability in a love relationship.

Most people unconsciously cling to their protective defenses until sufficient trust has formed and they can risk exposure without them. This may take a little time. The couple therapist's initial task is to help each individual in the couple to come out from behind his or her defenses and begin working on tolerating emotional vulnerability in sessions with each other.

Once intimate sharing starts to take the place of defensiveness in sessions, the couple therapist begins to invite to mutual consciousness the unhealthy relationship experiences both individuals endured that taught them the unhealthy beliefs, behavior and feelings that get played out in their love relationship. Their individual relationship experiences, what they learned from them, and how they became defensive to cope, are identified in each other's presence. As these revelations continue the level of intimate communication that is possible in the couple increases.

They each learn about each other's psychological love life, so that it is now possible to help each person identify when past unhealthy relationship experience is contaminating the love they feel for each other. Now there are two people working together to challenge their own and each other's unhealthy relationship experiences whenever they are being repeated and replicated in the relationship. From there, the couple with the help of the therapist, define which opposite healthy relationship experiences and learning they both need to create in their relationship to "correct" their unhealthy learning experiences earlier in life.

At times it will be possible to promote or simply support a healthy relationship experience two people have newly created and are experiencing together right in sessions. For example, when two people who grew up emotionally neglected and learned to use control and distance to avoid the anticipation of further neglect, drop the control and distance and risk moments of intimacy in sessions. At this stage in a couple therapy, healthy relationship experiences will also take place between sessions. The couple might report them in sessions and the therapist would be able to monitor the emerging corrective experiences taking place in their relationship. This is precisely how a love relationship can become an interpersonal experience of healing and growth for the two people involved.

CONCLUSION

It's Your Love Life!

Your love life belongs to you. Sounds like a pretty self-evident statement, right? Who else could your love life belong to anyway? Well, we've learned that your love life can belong to past experiences you've had, or even to someone else's love life experience. What that means is someone or something other than you is in charge of your love life. You could be replicating what you've learned from some experience you've had, or unconsciously following someone else's love life "script." This is never good. What happens in your particular love life should be entirely up to you. This "personalization" or "individualization" of your love life is one of the trademarks of a matured and satisfying adult life.

In this book I have described a method of owning your own love life. The first and most important step in this process is always the first one, when you *find out what you've learned about love relationships now you can do something about it.* The way unconscious emotional learning takes place in our lives, what you've learned about love relationships will initially be hidden even from you. But once you've become aware of what you've learned, you can decide to do something about it, if what you've learned is not healthy. The power to run your own love life is now being shifted back to you. Remember, once you know what you've learned, you can decide to change it or leave it alone. The choice is yours. The love life is yours. Take the time to find out what you've learned about love relationships from the love life experiences you've had in your life so far. The rewards are tremendous, for one, a better chance of finding and sustaining a healthy love relationship.

Take Control of Your Love Life

Let's review the steps in the process of taking control of your love life. Knowing what you've learned about love relationships in your life and how it determines your present and future love life experience is the first step. This knowledge starts the ball rolling in the direction of greater control over your love life. But just knowing is not enough to truly take control of your love life. The next two steps in this process involve what you are going to do with the information you now have. If you decide to go further, you'll want to decide whether what you've learned is healthy or unhealthy. If you decide it was unhealthy and it is not helping you find and sustain a healthy love relationship, you'll want to change what you've learned.

The next step in this process of getting control of your love life is to unlearn what you've learned. This is your first act of therapeutic defiance, *not going along with the unconscious learning program that has been operating in your internal psychological love life all these years.* Your next act of defiance is to do something different, but we'll get to that in a moment. Being brave enough to not only look at what you've personally learned about love relationships, and say no to unhealthy learning, is a real demonstration of your intention to take over the operation of this very important function in your life: your love life. You are now exercising your innate and inviolate ability to choose, once you are conscious of what you're choosing, along with your equally natural ability to change your mind. Yes, changing your psychological love life is really consciously changing your mind.

21ˢᵗ Century "Love Relationship Class"

The third and final step in this process of making a conscious change in your love life is to *do something different*. To choose to do something at odds with and opposed to the unhealthy unconscious lessons you've learned about how you should relate in a love relationship. Now the proverbial ball is rolling right back into your very own psychological hands. Once you start steering your love life in a healthier direction you are in control, often enough for the very first time as an adult person. You've decided it's time to learn something healthier for your love life.

The great thing about having this kind of control over your love life is you are now acutely aware that your experiences in life are natural teachers. With this in mind, you can go looking for the "corrective" experiences in your life that will teach you healthy lessons about love relationships. Based on an understanding of what went wrong the first time, you'll know what you need and go looking for love life experiences that will correct the particular unhealthy relationship experiences that contaminated your particular love life. It's hard to overstate the importance of this. You'll know what you need to "correct," when you've learned about your personal way of relating in love, in order to improve your chances of successfully finding and sustaining a healthy love relationship.

In fact, while writing this book I realized that I had unwittingly discovered the characteristics that are required to sustain a healthy love relationship as opposed to an unhealthy one. The list of unhealthy relationship experiences that are the cause of so much suffering in the love lives of my patients were not only important as specific prescriptions for change in individual cases, but their opposites are a *list of experiences needed to keep a love relationship healthy.* We had no idea going into this love life research that we would get to this point in our understanding. To remind you, the following opposites of the list of unhealthy relationship experiences are:

abandonment → **Attachment**

abuse → **Respect**

control → **Freedom**

dependency → **Independence**

dishonesty → **Honesty**

exploitation → **Consideration**

mistrust → **Trust**

neglect → **Devotion**

rejection → **Acceptance**

self-centeredness → **Intimacy**

To generate a faith in our ability to control our love lives and maximize the possibility of success, it's important to know what a healthy love relationship requires to keep it healthy. This list of healthy relationship experiences is the natural byproduct of research that has been initially and appropriately focused on the unhealthy love relationship. Conscious practicing of not only the experiences that correct the negative effects of specific unhealthy relationship experiences in our individual love lives, but also those experiences that keep a love relationship healthy in general is of inestimable value. To conclude this book, I'll speculate on just how each experience in this list of healthy relationship experiences has superseded the expectations of our research, along with a few love life recommendations and afterthoughts.

Attachment as an experience is vital to the formation and progression of a love relationship. It is the origin of commitment and reliability between two people. From its bond comes the depth that is possible when two people are committed to working out the kinks in their relationship. Kinks are the baggage all people bring with them to a love relationship along with the day to day differences between two people that are the spice and labor of love. To stay attached and working out differences permits the reward of a deepened love. Stay attached and working on the health of your love relationship, unless you are thoroughly convinced that leaving is necessary to find a better love life.

Respect is the clear recognition of another's value as a human being. This recognition is required for love to endure. When you respect the person you love, you understand the enrichment this particular individual brings to your life. Without respect, love dies. When a person values the love he or she has for another person, the person loved is respected as a consequence of that love. Practice respecting the person you love no matter what happens in your relationship and you will keep yourself free from the damage that can be done by disappointments and hurt that tempt some to devalue and abuse persons.

Freedom is the space to determine the course of your own life in or out of a love relationship. A free person gives the gift of love freely unhampered and unobstructed by unnecessary controls. If you are not loved freely you are not loved. You'll know that freedom exists in a love relationship when two people can be themselves in love. Being oneself means the freedom to be relaxed and spontaneous. Remember the poetic little saying, if you love someone set them free, if they love you back, it was meant to be. Set the person you fall in love with free. You can consider this your very first act of love in the relationship.

Independence is important in a love relationship because independence permits the existence of individuality in love. A healthy love relationship is like a huge umbrella under which two people are separate but together. Together but apart allows the room to grow unencumbered by the unwarranted dependency of another person. There is a certain amount of taking care of yourself that has to go on in a healthy love relationship. Just as there is a certain amount of taking care of the other person that goes on as well. The balance between these two defines the independence that is possible in a love relationship. Remember, independence means you are a whole person. When you are truly independent, no needed parts of you are given away to, or taken away by anyone.

Honesty is how two people get to know each other in love. It's the means by which two people locate each other in a relationship. Otherwise, lies and deception lead to confusion. If I don't know who you are, where you are, when you are, why you are, I don't know you. There is a guaranteed amount of vulnerability telling the truth on a consistent basis to someone you love. The possibility of rejection is real. Telling the truth when you don't know ahead of time what the reaction will be, is risky, to say the least. Sorry folks, that's the way it is in love. Honesty requires that we dispense with defense, tolerate vulnerability and take a risk on love's acceptance. Anything less is never healthy for love. When you fall in love, be honest and worry about it later, if you have to. Hopefully you won't have to.

Consideration means you have a sense of, a knowledge of, the "emotional needs" of the person you are in love with. In your love relationship, you are not doing things alone. You regularly and routinely check on the perspectives of the person you love regarding what is happening in the relationship. Consideration implies partnership. Two people creating a mutuality in their relationship. Co-creating their experiences together. Each considering the other. When you fall in love, show your consideration for the person you love regularly and routinely.

Trust is one of those experiences in love that is fundamental. You can't have love without trust. Without trust, you'll never get close enough to keep love alive. Without trust, you will never permit yourself to be vulnerable. Remember being vulnerable, or open as the substitute word, is required in order to give and receive love. In other words, if your heart is closed with mistrust, love has no access point. When you trust the person you love, you can sleep deeply in that person's presence. You can rest, relax, put your guard down, stop working so hard on being safe, and enjoy the love you are in. Given the collection of hurts that are possible in this world, practicing trust is a necessary step in keeping love alive in our love lives. This one will also require risks. Do your best. Healing is always possible if something goes wrong. Have faith in your natural ability to heal.

Devotion as the opposite of neglect is a full-time affair. You can't do devotion on a part-time basis like the part-time caring involved in neglect. Devotion is dedication on steroids. The person you are in love with is "special" and requires your devotion because of it. This is where the distinction between loving someone and "being in love" makes a difference. Because being in love is unique, so particular, so individualized, devotion is understandable. If and when someone matters that much to you, giving them everything you have makes sense. Devote yourself to the person you are in love with. If you are lucky, you'll get it back. Two people devoted to each other. Is there anything better in life?

Acceptance means the person you are in love with is OK, just the way he or she is, period. The period means you never try to change him or her. Being accepted is another one of those acts of love in a relationship. This one you feel, nice and direct. It's one thing to be able to be yourself with someone. It's another to know that the self you are being is accepted, fully and without reservation. Your love relationship then becomes a "home." A place to be yourself, relaxed, and accepted. An old friend of mine used to say, "What matters the most in love is to pick someone whose faults you can live with." Live with means accept. Check what you are accepting and not accepting in love. If you are accepting what you shouldn't, change that for a healthier love life. If you are not accepting what you should, change that for a healthier love life.

Last but not least, there is *intimacy*. The opposite of self-centeredness, otherwise known as narcissism among the psychoanalytic sophisticated. I prefer the term self-centered because it is a better descriptor of the problem. To be intimately in love is to change the "center" of your preoccupation from yourself to the self you are in love with. If you can't do that, for whatever personal reason, you are bound to be lonely in love. Technically, two people both centered on each other, means both people get centered in love. This is obviously one of the ways in which a love relationship is healing and healthy. Intimacy in love also implies presence. Being there for someone you are in love with. Close enough to see and be seen. Proximity is vital to the health and welfare of the love you are feeling. The next time you find yourself in love, get up close, as close as you can to the one you love.

Having successfully read this book, you've completed what I have come to consider the 21st century version of Buscaglia's "Love Class." Let's call my version the *"Love Relationship Class."* Since my focus is exclusively on the kind of relationship a person forms when he or she falls in love. When you take the time to become aware of what you've learned about love relationships in your love life, starting of course when you were born, you'll have the information you need to take control of your love life.

By now you should have realized, my cherished readers, that this whole enterprise depends upon being conscious of what you've learned about love relationships in your life. How can something this important be left to some unknown, repetitive, likely out of date experience you've once had? No way! Your love life is a vital and unbelievably important part of your psychological and physical life. Find out what's in it. Make it your own. Remember, it's your love life!

POSTSCRIPT: LOVE & GRIEF

We started this book off with a question: "What are the two most intense but normal human emotions?" *Love* and *grief* were the correct answers. This book focused on the type of relationship that promotes or negates a healthy love relationship. I would now like to say a few things about *grief* in comparison to love. First and foremost, these two emotions have a lot in common. In fact, I recently realized they are derived from the same place. A better way to say it is, *grief is the flipside of love*. How can that be? Grief as you recall is essentially what happens to love when the person, you are in love with, is no longer available. If you are going to fall in love, expect to grieve. Inevitably there will be a separation and there will be grief. Have I said anything you didn't know so far? OK, let's go further.

Love requires a relationship, whether it be with yourself or someone else. You should have learned this little bit of wisdom reading this book. Grief, on the other hand, is an emotion that occurs because a relationship has been lost. Therefore, the only thing grief requires is expression. Once expressed for as many times as needed, and it is usually not known beforehand how many times are needed, grief resolves. The resolution of grief leads naturally to enhanced memories, that means very high-definition memories of the person who has been grieved. They are "emotional memories." These emotional memories are available any time you wish to remember, like portable mental video, once the particular person has left you and grief has resolved.

Since unresolved grief, or unexpressed grief as we said earlier, is so common in a psychotherapy practice, it's quite easy to come to the conclusion that disappointments in love and unresolved grief over the course of a life time are responsible for a lion's share of mental illness.

Symptoms, disorders and syndromes all seem to evolve from the basic emotional problems of love life disappointments (starting at birth) and unresolved grief (grief never expressed for some reason or another). The added problem of converting grief to something else can make things a bit harder to figure out. From what I can tell, we humans do quite a bit of converting. Unresolved grief can be converted to anger, rage, heightened frustration, or something else. The point is, it is no longer grief and will be harder to resolve.

The implicit importance of grief is that it ultimately heals the heart. It repairs our ability to give love and receive love, when the heart has been damaged by loss. The resolution of grief naturally generates a renewed faith in our ability to handle the hurts of love. Without this repair, falling in love will be much harder to tolerate. Grief as the flipside of love deserves its own research given its role in healing our ability to have love in our lives.

This network of ideas related to and associated with the experience of love in a relationship context has never stopped evolving. It's been that way from the beginning, when I first began digging into this topic area with the psychological tools of an interpersonal psychoanalyst. Let's see what happens next was always in my mind. I'm not ready to stop asking the questions and expecting the answers. I still believe, perhaps even more so than before, that understanding love and love relationships is the true solution to our problems.

Dr. Thomas Jordan

New York City

2019

INDEX

REFERENCES

Buber, M. *I and Thou*. New York, NY: Charles Scribner & Sons, 1958.

Buscaglia, L. *Love*. New York, NY: Fawcett Columbine, 1972.

Buscaglia, L. *Living, Loving & Learning*. New York, NY: Fawcett Columbine, 1982.

Buscaglia, L. *Loving Each Other: The Challenge of Human Relationships*. New York, NY: Fawcett Columbine, 1984.

Buscaglia, L. *Born for Love: Reflections on Loving*. New York, NY: Fawcett Columbine, 1992.

Jordan, T. *Individuation in Contemporary Psychoanalysis: The Emergence of Individuality in Interpersonal & Relational Theory & Practice*. Springfield, IL: C.C. Thomas, 1999.

Jordan, T. *Healthy Love Relationship*. New York, NY: Vook, 2014.

Jurkovic, G.J. *Lost Childhoods: The Plight of the Parentified Child*. New York, NY: Routledge, 1997.

Lamons, B.N. *Habit, Education, and the Democratic Way of Life: The Vital Role of Habit in John Dewey's Philosophy of Education*. University of South Florida: Doctoral Dissertation, 2012.

Mahler, M. *On Human Symbiosis and the Vicissitudes of Individuation*.

New York, NY: International Universities Press, 1968.

Mahler, M., Pine, F., & Bergman, A. *The Psychological Birth of the Human Infant: Symbiosis and Individuation.* New York, NY: Basic Books, 1975.

Wolstein, B. *Freedom to Experience: A Study of Psychological Change from a Psychological Point of View.* New York, NY: Grune & Stratton, 1964.

Wolstein, B. *Theory of Psychoanalytic Therapy.* New York, NY: Grune & Stratton, 1967.

Wolstein, B. *Human Psyche in Psychoanalysis: The Development of Three Models of Psychoanalytic Psychotherapy.* Springfield, IL: Charles C. Thomas, 1971.

BIOGRAPHY

D r. Thomas Jordan is a clinical psychologist and psychoanalyst in private practice on the upper west side of Manhattan. He is a graduate of the New York University's Postdoctoral Program in Psychoanalysis, Clinical Associate Professor of Psychology, and a faculty member of the post-doctoral program. Dr. Jordan is the creator of the Love Life Webinar, author of "Learn to Love," "Healthy Love Relationship," and "Individuation in Contemporary Psychoanalysis," and co-founder of the lovelifelearningcenter.com. Dr. Jordan specializes in the treatment of chronic love life problems. He is in a group practice with his wife, Victoria Jordan LCSW, an experienced psychotherapist and couple therapist. Dr. Jordan has been researching and treating unhealthy love lives for 30 years.